BRITISH ENTERTAINERS IN FRANCE

SCENE FROM LESAGE'S "ARLEQUIN, ROI DE SERENDIB," AT THE FOIRE DE SAINT-GERMAIN, 1713

British Entertainers

in France

VICTOR LEATHERS

University of Toronto Press

Copyright, Canada, 1959, by
University of Toronto Press
Printed in Canada
London: Oxford University Press
Reprinted in 2018
ISBN 978-1-4875-8150-3 (paper)

A

MLLE CÉLINE AGNÈS BALLU

Hommages affectueux

Preface

British Entertainers in France is not a study of international literary relationships. It presents a record of visits to France by British entertainers and, where possible, reports their reception by the critics, the artists, and the public. Speculation as to influence is indulged in only where influence seems to have been apparent and indisputable. For various reasons, no survey is made of one category of entertainers, that of musicians. Nor is there any discussion of the small and ephemeral English troupes which occasionally played for the British colonies at Boulogne and Calais in the eighteenth and nineteenth centuries.

To my colleague Professor R. N. Hallstead I wish to indicate my hearty appreciation of his invaluable help at critical points in the preparation of this book. My thanks are also due to the Humanities Research Council of Canada for a grant facilitating research in France and for advice regarding the manuscript.

Mention of Professor J. L. Borgerhoff's volume *Le Théâtre anglais à Paris sous la Restauration* is in order and I should like to acknowledge my debt to him. When discussing the 1827-8 season, I was both aided and embarrassed by this thoroughly scholarly work. For my chapter on the Penley visit I may claim quite independent treatment. As a matter of principle I scrupulously avoided using such citations as Professor Borgerhoff had selected except in one or two cases where factual statements such as the initial Penley announcement were involved. In certain cases I differ with his findings but have not attempted to argue the case, simply presenting my own facts and interpretations. With regard to the visit of 1827-8 I continued the policy of independent research as far as possible. My chief debt to Professor Borgerhoff lies in the fact that I was able to utilize his splendid tabulations of performances and his detailed reports on the textual treatment of Shakespeare's plays. In this chapter too I refrain from discussing minor differences of opinion and simply state my findings. In view of the fact that Professor Borgerhoff's work is devoted to a limited field while the present study covers a very broad one, it is inevitable that my treatment of the 1827-8 season should be briefer and less detailed than his.

I would finally offer my most grateful acknowledgments to the University of Toronto Press for the generosity of its Publications Fund, to Miss Francess G. Halpenny, its Editor, whose editorial counsel and encouragement have been deeply valued, and to Miss Barbara Ham whose reading of the copy greatly aided in the final preparation of the manuscript.

V.L.

Contents

	PREFACE	vii
1	Prelude, with Variations	3
2	Battle Royal	8
3	On with the Dance	17
4	"Cut the Dialect and Come to the 'Osses"	26
5	The Pleasures of a Year and the Follies of a Day	37
6	Beauty and the Beast	47
7	"Once More Unto the Breach . . ."	58
8	Shakespeare, Smithson, Shore, and Company	69
9	Anticlimax	93
10	"Well Have We Done, Thrice Valiant Countrymen"	102
11	History Repeats Itself	115
12	Here Come the Clowns!	126
13	Tumblers and Talkers, a Fool and Footitt	141
14	The Why and Wherefore	155
	APPENDIX	167
	BIBLIOGRAPHY	170
	INDEX	175

BRITISH ENTERTAINERS IN FRANCE

1 · Prelude, with Variations

British entertainers have been going abroad for a long time; English actors, we find, visited the continent in the retinues of ecclesiastics as early as 1414 when they played before the bishops assembled at the Council of Constance.[1] Visits to France in this period, however, differ in two respects from those to other countries. No patronage seems to have existed for these appearances, and the earliest visits occurred considerably later than those to other parts of Europe.

The first appearance of British entertainers in France came in 1583 when Paris was visited by a troupe of acrobats, possibly the same English *volteadors* seen in the French capital towards the close of the century with a Spanish company. These tumblers frequently joined forces with such native popular entertainers as the famous Gaultier Garguille.[2] No doubt the English and Spanish visitors, doubly foreign, would have an added attraction for audiences accustomed to strolling Italian players.

In Paris a monopoly of the drama was held at this time by the Confrérie de la Passion. They were forbidden to present sacred themes; periodically, however, and under some difficulties, they staged profane mysteries and farces. To the various difficulties of the Confrérie was added in 1598 a troublesome affair with one Jehan Sehais, described as a *comédien anglais*. In May, Sehais hired the Hôtel de Bourgogne from the Confrérie for theatrical representations as permitted by the regulations. Soon after, he attempted to evade his obligation of one *écu* per day and by order of the Châtelet was expelled from the Hôtel de Bourgogne. Undaunted, Sehais continued performances outside the theatre. The irate Confrères appealed once more to the court which again pronounced against the visitors.

June 4 1598. Verdict of the Châtelet given in favour of the said Confrérie against the said players with regard to the above mentioned rental of one *écu* per day, the said English playing elsewhere than in the said Hôtel de Bourgogne.[3]

[1] A. W. Ward, *A History of English Literature* (London, 1899), I, p. 471.
[2] E. Fournier, *La Chanson de Gaultier Garguille* (Paris, 1858), p. lix.
[3] Eudore Soulié, *Recherches sur Molière et sur sa famille* (Paris, 1863), p. 153.

At this point the troupe disappears from Paris and from literary history.

We discover English players in France again during 1604, this time when a Shakespearean play was presented at the court of Henri IV. The scanty particulars about them come from the private journal of Jean Héroard, tutor of the Dauphin. Under date of September 18, he describes the reaction of little Louis, then only three years of age, whom he had "brought into the main hall to hear a tragedy given by some English actors. He listened to them with patient grave composure until one of the characters had to be beheaded." Three days later the prince "got into costume with his apron as a head dress and a white scarf, and imitated the English actors who were at the court and whom he had seen act." The following day Louis again insisted on playing at acting. "'Sir,' I said, 'what do you say?' He answers, 'Tiph, taph,' in a loud voice." Later in the evening he treated his mother to a short exhibition. Finally, the following Sunday, he again demanded *la comédie*. "He said, 'Let us get dressed.' They put on his apron as a head dress; he began to talk, saying, 'Tiph, taph, milord,' and striding up and down."[4]

Which of Shakespeare's plays was viewed by the court? The most plausible suggestion would seem to be the second part of *Henry IV*. The "Tiph, taph, milord" was probably the little Dauphin's version of Falstaff's remark in Act II, at the close of scene i, to the Chief Justice and Gower: "This is the right fencing grace, my lord; tap for tap, and so part fair." The choice of *Henry IV* may have been intended as a compliment to the bluff King of Navarre, Henri IV of France.

Four years later, in 1608, a Scotsman named Banks appeared on the Rue Saint Jacques in Paris with his remarkable trained horse, Morocco, "the dancing horse" to which Shakespeare refers in *Love's Labor's Lost*. In Montlyard's memoirs we find a lengthy account of Banks' performances at the Lyon d'Argent inn. The horse retrieved objects, walked on its hind legs, and distinguished various colours; or "his master tosses him a glove and bids him get it and carry it to the person in the crowd wearing glasses, for example." In one sketch, Morocco proved lazy and his master threatened to sell him. The horse, with every evidence of despondency, lay down to die. Then, when someone in the crowd begged for pardon, Morocco revived, and trotted over to thank his defender.

[4]Jean Héroard, *Journal de Jean Héroard sur l'enfance et la jeunesse de Louis XIII (1601–1628)* (Paris, 1868), I, pp. 88 ff.

The best of it was that the Magistrate, concluding that this was impossible without magic, had the Scotsman imprisoned and the horse locked up. But later, recognizing that it was all done by commands and signals, he had him released and allowed him to exhibit his horse.[5]

At Orléans, Banks again found himself accused of sorcery, and his ingenious method of clearing himself by means of his fellow actor is related by a contemporary.

He ordered his horse to seek out one in the press of the people who had a crucifix on his hat; which done he bade him kneel down unto it, and not this only, but also to rise up again and kiss it. "And now gentlemen" (quoth he) "I think my horse hath acquitted both me and himself"; and so his adversaries rested satisfied; conceiving (as it might seem) that the devil had no power to come near the cross.[6]

Ben Jonson in *The Famous Voyage* gives a burlesque account of Banks being burned as a sorcerer, which probably came from a garbled version of the Orléans incident:

> Old Bankes the juggler, our Pythagoras,
> Grave tutor to the learned horse. Both which
> Being, beyond sea, burned for one witch:
> Their spirits transmigrated to a cat . . .

However, Mr. Banks' subsequent appearances in England comfortably disprove this unfortunate dénouement.

The dramatic activity in French colleges of the Scottish savant Buchanan might seem to merit study; Buchanan, however, figures in French circles as a Latinist who trained his students in the presentation of Latin adaptations from classical plays. But there were other scholars from the British Isles who did offer plays in English performed by English-speaking actors. These were professors of Jesuit colleges in Paris, Douai, and Saint Omer, whose senior boys from time to time presented quite remarkable productions.

The records of Saint Omer are the most impressive. From 1602 until its closing in 1762, plays seem to have been presented frequently, although after 1676 large gaps occur in the records. The professors who prepared the plays usually wrote in Latin or French, but occasionally followed a Shakespearean pattern and at times wrote in English. Texts,

---

[5]Cited by Arthur Christian, *Etudes sur le Paris d'autrefois, VIIe série, Les Jeux équestres* (Paris, 1907), p. 146. (Montlyard is the pseudonym of J. D. Dralymont.)
[6]Cited by Thomas Frost, *The Old Showmen and the Old London Fairs* (London, 1870), pp. 23 ff.

reports of presentation, or a bare mention of title remain for almost a hundred plays. These were chiefly Biblical scenes or lives of the saints, but classical and historical topics were also treated. All were moral in intent, serious and frequently tragic in tone. The presentations took place before kindly but critical audiences of professors, parents, and notable visitors. The prohibition against women on the stage necessitated some dexterity on the part of authors and producers; but on the whole both plays and ballets were creditably interpreted. But though these plays may have been interesting in themselves, such cloistered productions can scarcely have exerted any influence on the theatre of France.[7]

The restoration of the Stuarts in 1660 established especially cordial relations between England and France and increased the theatrical exchange. This was, however, largely one-way, in visits to London by French artists. Thomas Betterton, the leading English actor and manager of the day, did visit France three times, but on each occasion he went as an official theatrical purveyor to Charles II and not to perform. At the royal request Betterton visited Paris in 1662 to examine the French theatre; this task bore much fruit especially in English imitations of Molière. A decade later Charles again sent him abroad just prior to the opening of the Dorset Garden Theatre: the new playhouse, when opened, proved to be fitted in exact imitation of the French theatres and Opéra. Finally, in 1683, Betterton revisited Paris to arrange for the importation of French operas and to bring back a company of dancers who were to lead celebrations at the English court.[8]

Only one notable English actor of this period visited France as a performer. He was that extraordinary being, Joe Haynes, probably the most gifted and popular comedian who ever appeared in England. Remarkable as were his exploits on the stage he quite eclipsed them by his impertinent association with the nobility of the day both in England and in France. In the latter, this irrepressible prankster regularly posed as a count, ran heavily into debt, and was even threatened with arrest for his misbehaviour.

---

[7]Those wishing an exhaustive treatment of this subject are referred to the following volumes: Ernest Boysse, *Le Théâtre des Jésuites* (Paris, 1880), and G. Hautecloque, *Les Représentations dramatiques dans les collèges de l'Artois* (Abbeville, 1888).

[8]R. W. Lowe, *Betterton* (London, 1891), *passim*.

Haynes appeared on the French stage before Louis XIV in the première of *Le Bourgeois Gentilhomme*, October 14, 1670. His success is reported in the dispatches of William Perwick, a British civil servant, who wrote on October 25:

The King will be (here I mean) at St. Germain this day to see the Dolphin [sic] upon whose indisposition the king broke up all his *divertissements* in the very midst to come away. I think I told you something of Jo Haynes; now I can add that he has behaved himself to everybody's wonder & diverted the king by several English dances to his great satisfaction and that of all the court. I believe he will have a present made him. If you should think it convenient it would do him a great kindness in England to mention him in the Gazette among the King's *divertissements* at Chambort, [sic] where whilst the balet [sic] were preparing, he hunted the wild bore [sic] and pheasants. By the enclosed you see the several entries & manner of the balet; between every one Haynes had orders to dance by himself, and notwithstanding the confronting of the best dancers carried it off to admiration & was ordered to dance some things twice over.[9]

The next year Haynes was a member of Betterton's company, playing the role of the French master in Ravenscroft's adaptation of *Le Bourgeois Gentilhomme* entitled *Mamamouchi, or the Citizen Turned Gentleman*. In this part his first-hand observations would stand him in good stead. That same year he was sent to France by Charles II to engage in professional observation similar to that of Betterton. In Paris, between expensive bouts of roistering, he examined especially the complicated machinery of the French operatic spectacles.

A few fleeting appearances of strolling players in the French provinces occur in the later years of the seventeenth century. (A list of these passing appearances may be found in the Appendix.) But more continuous and more significant elements of our subject now command attention.

[9] *The Dispatches of Wm. Perwick, English Agent in Paris*, edited for the Royal Historical Society (London, B. Curran, ed., 1903).

2 · Battle Royal

During the first half of the eighteenth century English performers in France are particularly interesting and important because of their close association with the development of three new types of entertainment, and their intimate participation in one of the fiercest and most prolonged struggles in theatrical history. The story of these visitors cannot, however, be properly presented without retracing the lengthy skirmishing between the actors of the Théâtre Français and the popular entertainers or *acteurs forains* of the Paris fairs.

The fairs of Saint Laurent and Saint Germain, dating from mediaeval times, were of a dual nature, being both commemorative and commercial. Saint Laurent owed its founding by Louis le Gros to an act of royal penance; the profits of the gathering were to be used in masses for the king's soul. In the early seventeenth century, it had taken definite form with a site in the Faubourg Saint Denis, an annual duration of three months, and direction by the monastery of Saint Lazare. The fair spread over several acres, its wooden buildings in ordered rows, and its stalls rented to responsible merchants on an annual basis.

On the south side of the Seine, the Abbey of Saint Germain des Prés had from time immemorial exercised the right to hold an annual fair between the Latin Quarter and the aristocratic suburb of Saint Germain. Although under the auspices of an abbey, this fair differed from Saint Laurent in being a *foire franche* or free fair. This meant that the conditions of commercial participation were much less rigorous; indeed, the only prohibitions were those against books and weapons. This liberty was important, since it opened the way to participants offering not goods but entertainment. Saint Laurent, being essentially commercial, attracted a serious bourgeois clientele in search of provisions and household equipment. Saint Germain, on the contrary, by its location and its offerings attracted a much more varied public, made up of university students ready for town-and-gown brawling, members of the upper class in search of excitement, and even the more raffish elements of the nobility looking for popular distractions.

The attractions of the Saint Germain fair at first consisted mainly of cafés and cabarets, frequently called *guinguettes*. But as the century advanced a variety of entertainment appeared. By tradition the tumblers, tightrope dancers, and acrobats held priority at the fairs. With these, however, came the sleight-of-hand men and jugglers, and the exhibitors of curiosities, of monsters, and of trained or exotic animals. Despite the disorders which arose from the presence of such elements, they attracted great numbers of people to the benefit of the merchants. So obvious did this become, that the Saint Laurent authorities felt compelled to admit the tumblers, the dancers, and the *guinguettes* also. Since the Confrérie de la Passion still held rigorous control of all public presentations in the capital, the fairs represented the sole refuge for independent actors and especially for the strolling players.

The physical conditions under which the *forains* appeared were not much superior to their legal status. Their plays were given in what they called loges, which are described in the *Mémoires* of the Parfait brothers.

A loge was an enclosed space . . . where platforms were set up for the performances, a tight rope for the dancers, and a platform not more than a foot and a half high for the acrobats, quite without ornament or decoration. After each fair everything in the loge was put away to be used at the next one.[1]

Less than twenty years later, more ambitious facilities appeared: a well-raised, properly lighted stage, padded seats, some attempt at decoration, provision for a small orchestra, and considerable stage equipment. These structures remained as permanent properties.

The entertainment offered by these companies towards the end of the seventeenth century made its appeal at the most popular level. The earliest example extant of the plays given at the fairs, *Les Forces de l'amour et de la magie*, appeared in February, 1678.[2] Produced by two celebrated dancers, Charles Alard and Maurice Vondrebecke, it included a curious mixture of brief dialogues, *tableaux vivants*, comic interludes, acrobatics, and scenic effects. Brief as it is, the dialogue of the

[1] C. and F. Parfait, *Mémoires pour servir à l'histoire de la foire* (Paris, 1743), I, p. 3.
[2] For the complete text of this play see E. d'Auriac, *Le Théâtre de la foire* (Paris, 1878), pp. 57 ff.

three principal characters does present a story and reveal a suggestion of characterization, while Merlin, the servant, leaves a moral thought in the phrase: "Tout par amitié rien par la force." "The play," we are told, "was presented by a company of twenty-four dancers of various countries, the most brilliant who have ever appeared in France."[3]

The dancers took definite roles and are often described as actors. (Indeed, to interpret references to such performers throughout the eighteenth century correctly, it must be realized that the terms *danseur*, *sauteur*, and *danseur de corde* [or tightrope acrobat] became at times so vague as to indicate almost any member of a company presenting ballets, *divertissements*, or pantomimes, and this was especially true when they were used to indicate the actors of the fairs.) That English performers were among the dancers for this company is altogether likely in view of their reputation. In his *Histoire générale de la danse*, Jacques Bonnet, a contemporary, comments: "I have never in my travels seen more daring and skilful dancers than the English, the Turks, and the Chinese,"[4] and of these groups the English would obviously be the easiest for French directors to recruit. *Les Forces* enjoyed great popularity and when, by royal command, it was presented before Louis XIV, His Majesty granted Alard permission to continue playing.[5] From the elements found in this play there developed most of the varied forms of the *spectacles de la foire* over the next century.

The first development was a tendency, natural in such loosely knit works, to offer type figures, the Pierrots and Harlequins, Columbines and Pantaloons, Scaramouches and Trivelins of the *commedia dell'arte* as created by the Italian players at the Hôtel de Bourgogne. When Louis XIV suppressed the Italians in 1697 for their satire on Mme de Maintenon, the *acteurs forains* thereupon appropriated much of their repertoire.[6] The public, which regretted the absence of the Italians, flocked to the fairs in steadily increasing numbers. Indeed, the popularity of the *forains* became so great that the players of the Théâtre Français persuaded the government to prohibit dramatic presentations at the fairs. The popular entertainers retaliated by presenting detached scenes, with interludes of dancing by English and other foreign troupes. After some bewilderment, the audiences became used to the new form

[3]D'Auriac, *Le Théâtre de la foire*, p. 22.
[4]J. Bonnet, *Histoire générale de la danse* (Paris, 1721), p. 57.
[5]P. Fromageot, *La Foire Saint Germain* (Paris, n.d.), p. 24.
[6]A. Heulhard, *La Foire Saint Laurent* (Paris, 1878), p. 191.

and supported these disjointed plays. Then, in 1706, the Comédiens Français managed to obtain a prohibition of all dialogue on the stages of the fairs. The *forains* thereupon gave monologues with replies from the wings, or pantomimed responses, or dialogues from opposite wings. The novelty, even grotesqueness, of these subterfuges continued to attract the crowds, and the Comédiens next demanded and obtained the elimination of all spoken parts. Desperate, the actors of Saint Germain and Saint Laurent none the less found yet another answer to their enemies. And their answer was of considerable importance theatrically, for it consisted of the invention and the development of two new theatrical types, the *opéra comique* and the *vaudeville*.

The former originated in the mind of a quick-witted woman. In 1708 the widow of Maurice Vondrebecke conceived the idea of putting her troupe under the wing of the Royal Academy of Music (that is, the Opéra) by obtaining from the Academy permission to include in her presentations changes of scenery, special dances, and, most important of all, singers. Thus fulfilling the letter of the law which forbade spoken dialogue, the company carried on with impunity. However, Mme Vondrebecke's remarriage gave an opportunity for the cancellation of the privilege in 1710, and it was promptly taken. Reduced to utter silence, the *acteurs forains* continued to resist and soon presented what were called *pièces muettes* or *pièces à écriteaux*. In these the actors supplemented their dumb-show by printed speeches, which they drew from one pocket, displayed before the crowd, and then placed in the opposite pocket. A considerable improvement on this hampering procedure was the use of large streamers held above the players by boys suspended at each side of the stage. The larger lettering and the freedom thus afforded the actors for stage business made this innovation highly popular with the public.

The second new type developed when the streamer dialogue was replaced by couplets drawn from familiar songs, or including topical references and set to familiar airs. The important innovation was the participation of the audience by means of these couplets, commonly called *vaudevilles*. They were familiar to everyone; their refrains and many repetitions made it easy to carry a crowd along in the singing of them. Given the air by the tiny orchestra permitted by the regulations, and primed by a few professionals among them, the audience sang the couplets and thus had a share in the play. The introduction of satirical comment and spirited topical allusions into the verses naturally added to their piquancy, and the audiences thoroughly relished them.

A rebellious attitude, *l'esprit frondeur*, characterized early eighteenth-century society in France, and these actors catered readily to it, with the result that the *spectacles de la foire* were consistently satirical in nature. An amusing example of this spirit is furnished by the final weapon of the harassed entertainers. Forbidden to use words, they at times fell back upon inarticulate gibberish, which so exactly imitated the delivery and intonation of well-known artists in the state troupes as to provide not only something of the narrative of the play being presented, but also a ludicrous parody of the style and mannerisms of their enemies the Comédiens Français.[7]

Intimately connected with these struggles was an Englishman, Richard Baxter, whose name is prominently associated with some of the most important troupes during the first two decades of the century. He is first encountered in 1707, playing in collaboration with Louis Nivellon, a remarkable pantomime dancer. A battered hand-bill of 1709 advertising Nivellon's production remains extant, and in it the dancer-manager announces that:

> with permission of the King and of the Lieutenant-General of Police, his troupe together with his English associates, have prepared for the public, during the remainder of the Saint Germain fair several comic scenes of an extraordinary nature which he feels sure will be admired.[8]

Baxter collaborated with Nivellon not only as the leader of an English group but also as a distinguished performer. In the plays he regularly took the role of Harlequin, a character which in these productions traditionally fell to the leading actor.

The Harlequin of eighteenth-century French pantomime must not be thought of as the cowardly, gluttonous, somewhat lewd valet of the original Italian type. With the other Italian figures, more so than many of them since he was the main figure, Harlequin took on French characteristics, particularly that of sparkling wit. It could be argued

---

[7] The story of the struggle between the *comédiens* and the *forains* has been treated frequently from various points of view. The best discussions are those by MM. Albert Maurice, Eugène d'Auriac, Arthur Heulhard, and Pierre Fromageot. A recent book on the history of the character Harlequin, by Thelma Niklaus, also gives a very lively account of the matter. Contemporary writers were regularly descriptive rather than interpretive in their approach.

[8] P. Fromageot, *La Foire Saint Germain*, displays a facsimile reproduction of this bill facing page 38.

that, in the hands of authors like Lesage and Fuzelier, he became the early eighteenth-century link between the wily valets of Molière and the adroit Figaro of Beaumarchais.

Baxter remained with Nivellon until 1711, giving great satisfaction with his performances. Unfortunately, Nivellon's capacities as manager fell short of his gifts as a dancer; during the season of 1711 at the Saint Germain fair, he was forced to disband his company. The chief members, including Baxter and his close friend and associate Saurin, transferred to the Baron players. Baron died shortly afterward and the following year his widow reorganized the company. To avoid pursuit for her husband's debts, she placed the organization in the name of her two leading actors, Saurin (or Sorin) and Baxter and the company then bore the official title of Le Nouvel Opéra Comique de Baxter et de Sorin. Baxter's capacity as a performer was, of course, fully recognized, and rival companies were eager for his services; this would suggest that his appearance as one of the public sponsors of the troupe meant more than the provision of a mere name behind which Mme Baron really directed the theatre. Baxter would certainly never have consented to become a cat's-paw for a woman with whom the majority of people found it very difficult to deal.

From 1712 to 1716, Baxter aided in the management of the Nouvel Opéra and enjoyed a series of personal theatrical triumphs, particularly at the Saint Laurent fair. During these five seasons he is recorded as appearing in an unbroken series of successful presentations from the complete repertoire of his group. He performed excellently in the *pièces à écriteaux* or streamer dialogue plays which he enlivened with his comic pantomime. He danced the Harlequin role in half a dozen *opéras comiques*, some of these being obvious caricatures of current successes at the Opéra. He led the crowds in singing the satirical couplets, the *vaudevilles*, with which these productions were interspersed. And his sprightly performances in the *divertissements* evoked special applause from the crowds.[9]

These *divertissements*, a mixture of dancing and singing, came as a tradition from the performances of the *danseurs de corde*. Later they also became a parody of the operatic ballet. The *divertissements* were

[9] Baxter's performances across these years are set forth in the *Mémoires* of the Parfait brothers, vol. I, *passim*, and also in Emile Campardon, *Les Spectacles de la foire* (Paris, 1877), I (under Baxter).

presented regularly at the ends of acts or of plays, never as part of the plays themselves. They were not pantomimes, but simply gay interludes. The combination of Harlequin play and *divertissement* is worth noting. For in the development of the ballet-pantomime by English artists towards 1740, it was precisely this linking of Harlequin play and *divertissement* which produced a form ideally suited to the pantomimists who visited Paris at that period.

Striking proof of Baxter's stature as artist and manager appears in the fact that the three outstanding librettists of the fairs, Fuzelier, Dorneval, and Lesage, collaborated with him. These authors among them produced almost all the scenarios and libretti for the company. Of the first two little need be said, except that their services were keenly sought after by the other *forain* companies. It is more interesting to find the future author of *Gil Blas* regularly furnishing scripts for the English artist's troupe.

Unfortunately, the Comédiens Français were again preparing an attack, this time with reinforcements. In 1716 the restrictions against the Italians were removed, and these actors joined the Royal players against the *forains*, who during the twenty-year ban had appropriated the characters, and indeed the repertoire, of the Italian company. The combined onslaught resulted in such oppressive regulations that the Baxter and Saurin troupe disbanded and scattered.

The two directors first visited England, where they appeared at Drury Lane in April, 1716, as a highly touted pair of artists "lately arrived from Paris."[10] They gave a Harlequin and Scaramouche dance drawn from *The Whimsical Death of Harlequin* and also *La Guinguette, or Harlequin Turned Tapster*. Apparently Baxter felt more at home in France; he and his comrade returned to that country and toured the provinces as strolling actors. In 1721, the two came back to Paris and undertook the formation of a theatre of *opéra comique* at the Saint Laurent fair. But, in spite of their combined experience and energy, the project failed completely before the end of the season. This reverse was not altogether attributable to the theatrical competition. For some five years, from 1717 onward, all the Paris theatres suffered heavily from the mania for gambling and wild speculation which seized the capital, a mania which not only ruined many of the patrons of the theatres, but also heavily involved the government itself. Disgusted at

[10] M. W. Disher, *Clowns and Pantomimes* (London, 1925), p. 229.

the unfortunate outcome of his venture, and probably weary after twenty years of strenuous theatrical life, Baxter withdrew completely from the theatre and retired to a monastery.[11]

Of handsome face and figure, and gifted as dancer, actor and mimic, Baxter showed particular skill in satire and parody. At the height of the battle between the Royal players and the *acteurs forains*, a regular procedure at the fairs was to ape the pompous declamation, posturing, or dancing of the more noted members of the royal troupes. Baxter created a sensation with his droll imitation, in woman's dress, of Mlle Prévot, who was being loudly applauded at the Opéra for her dance entitled *Le Caprice*. The Englishman also excelled in his *lazzi*, that is, the brief interludes of pantomime clowning between the speeches, *écriteaux*, or couplets. These comic turns were intended not only to give the audience time to catch up mentally with the main action, but also to give other actors a few moments for improvisations of the *commedia dell'arte* description.

This artist's relationship with his chief playwright was to be of literary importance. Lesage's début as a writer for the Saint Laurent productions began a long association with the fairs by that great observer of eighteenth-century France, and this association cannot be dismissed lightly. In his work for the Baxter company the author of *Turcaret* and *Le Diable Boiteux* was enabled not merely to vent his spleen at the shabby treatment accorded him by the Royal theatres prior to 1712, but also to develop his powers of observation and satirical comment. There is no question that Lesage's début at Saint Germain was greatly facilitated by his excellent English interpreter.[12] All his earlier pieces were written especially for Baxter and centred closely around the Harlequin role, which the Englishman handled superbly. The success of the Nouvel Opéra Comique from 1712 to 1716 came from the happy combination of a new type of material to manipulate, a writer capable of improving it, and a fine artist able to bring the writer's creations to life on the stage.

The role of Harlequin at the fairs declined in importance following Baxter's retirement, in all probability because there was not another outstanding interpreter to replace him. This decline is easily established by an examination of the titles of the offerings through the twenties

[11] Parfait and Parfait, *Mémoires*, I, p. 118.
[12] V. Barbaret, *Lesage et le théâtre de la foire* (Nancy, 1877), pp. 41 ff.

and thirties. On the other hand, the Pierrot role assumed a greater importance with the appearance of several remarkable Pierrots, particularly the brilliant artist Hamoche. Again, the Harlequin part revived towards 1740 when a large number of English players were performing at the fairs.[13]

Baxter must be granted even higher rank than that of a gifted actor. In the battle between the monopoly-holding Comédiens and the *forains*, the frequent appearance of his name in sheriff's documents proves that he was a protagonist of considerable courage and stature. Under date of September 10, 1714, for example, Sieur Etienne Milache, *comédien ordinaire du Roi*, made an official complaint that, in defiance of various verdicts and regulations forbidding the *forains*

> to play or have played or represented on public theatres any play or comedy in the form of dialogues, colloquies, monologues or in any other manner whatsoever, under the designated penalties, including demolition of the theatres; nonetheless Messrs. Sorin and Baxter, their associates and other directors in defiance of the said verdicts continue to play and present publicly and daily, plays and comedies in the environs of the Foire Saint Laurent in which plays the actors and actresses speak to each other, and reply in prose according to the nature of the comic play which they are presenting, which forms complete comedies and which is directly contrary to the above-mentioned regulations.[14]

In the circumstances it would seem an honour to be singled out as chief offender; Baxter must be accorded a place of significance for launching new theatrical types, the *vaudeville* and the *opéra comique*, and, as well, must be admired for his courage in the unequal battle against theatrical monopoly.

[13]*Ibid.*, p. 136.
[14]Court document cited by Emile Campardon, *Les Spectacles de la foire*, I (under Baxter).

3 · On with the Dance

The story of British entertainers at the fairs from Baxter's retirement until the disappearance of the fairs themselves is almost entirely that of the British pantomimes and ballets at the Opéra Comique. The government had given official status to this theatre in 1724, but the Théâtre Français on occasion managed to suppress the institution and the British productions actually replaced those of the Opéra. It was, nevertheless, rather when a flourishing Opéra Comique called for their collaboration that the foreign troupes prospered.

In 1726, however, an English actor, John Rinner, entered the theatrical world of Paris by constructing a *jeu de paume* or open-air theatre to stage his own productions.[1] He brought a company of dancers and pantomimists to the Saint Germain fair, but his chief attraction consisted of a troupe of marionettes with which he presented two highly popular parodies in the comic opera tradition. The authors of these works were the familiar trio, Fuzelier, Dorneval, and Lesage. To find a man of Lesage's reputation the literary servant of wooden dolls may seem surprising, but it was not strange at this period when the creation and manipulation of these substitute actors had been brought to a high point of excellence. *Forain* producers regularly held the marionettes as reserve forces and on occasion used them as a last line of defence, since they were not usually attacked by the Comédiens Français. The puppets also provided a front behind which surreptitious performances by live actors were given. Rinner was not then introducing any novelty, but rather continuing a tradition and insuring himself against harassment by monopoly. His distinctive contribution lay in the quality of his plays, and his theatre provided formidable competition for the Opéra Comique.[2]

During several succeeding years, the principal English figures at the fairs were individual artists of exceptional ability who appeared as

[1] C. and F. Parfait, *Mémoires pour servir à l'histoire de la foire* (Paris, 1743), II, p. 34. Also Charles Magnin, *Histoire des marionettes* (Paris, 1834), p. 160.
[2] E. d'Auriac, *Le Théâtre de la foire* (Paris, 1878), p. 43.

soloists or in small groups. Thus Restier's troupe of 1727 contained an English acrobat, unfortunately anonymous, whose tours de force left his audience gasping.[3] The next year the director of the Opéra Comique took care to bring a group of similar English performers whom he presented in the interludes of his operas.[4]

Throughout the Saint Laurent season of 1731 two English dancers, Renton and Haughton, teamed with the celebrated French mime Roger to perform a highly successful *divertissement* billed as *La Guinguette Anglaise*. A troupe of English dancers, to which Haughton and Renton belonged, were playing at the Saint Laurent fair that same year. Obviously this was a good company, for in September they were summoned to perform before the Queen at Versailles, after which they returned to complete the Saint Laurent season with their consistently popular *guinguette anglaise*.[5] This term, which was applied to many ballets over the first half of the century, indicated a conventional, even stereotyped, production representing all the popular ideas about the English, but containing stock figures similar to the earlier Italian types. Its loose arrangement allowed the inclusion of much *commedia dell'arte* improvisation by gifted performers.

During the middle thirties no mention of British visitors occurs. But from 1737 the English artists not only reappeared in force but also introduced a truly distinctive form of pantomime.

As has already been seen, the great English artist of the fairs, Richard Baxter, closely followed the French version of the *commedia dell'arte* in his handling of the Harlequin role, and in the numerous *lazzi* or comical turns sprinkled through his productions. He made no distinctively English contribution to the role; his Harlequinades were essentially those of the French *forain* entertainers of his day; that is to say, they depicted the exploits of a dominant personage, Harlequin, frisking through a series of fantastic, individual adventures. Little in the way of story was suggested by the skeletal scenarios or *canevas* on which these productions were based. The final resource of the artists lay in their own inventiveness and virtuosity. Baxter's retirement ended the dominance of Harlequin at the fairs, but actually from 1716 on the reorganized Italian troupe had, so to speak, repossessed Harlequin. Such brilliant interpreters of the role as Thomassin kept the

[3]Parfait and Parfait, *Mémoires*, II, p. 42.
[4]Maurice Albert, *Les Théâtres de la foire* (Paris, 1900), p. 162.
[5]Parfait and Parfait, *Mémoires*, II, pp. 69-75.

Harlequin tradition alive in modified form, although not, of course, at the fairs.[6] Even as Baxter was quitting the stage, however, another Englishman was inventing and popularizing in England not only a distinctive type of pantomime, but also an even more distinctive Harlequin.

In 1717, John Rich, son of the theatrical impresario Christopher Rich, found himself patentee of Lincoln's Inn Field theatre. This theatre was suffering from unpopularity, and Rich found it necessary to hit on a device which would attract attention. His solution was to develop the role of Harlequin as a personal specialty. Few Englishmen had done anything with Harlequin. Joe Haynes had tried him in Ravenscroft's *Scaramouche* of 1667, and the dancing master, John Weaver, had used him in two indifferently received plays early in the eighteenth century. But Rich, both as author and as actor, created an English Harlequin of unique and striking nature. Forced into comic roles by his unprepossessing face and virtual illiteracy he found his true vocation in interpreting the mute masked Italian comic. Beginning at first as simply a graceful dancing Harlequin, he steadily developed remarkable capacity in mime.

Rich was not, however, content to dance his way through trivial productions; his pantomimes proved to be as original as his Harlequin. Garrick's biographer, Davies, gives details of Rich's English-style pantomime:

> To retrieve the credit of his theatre, Rich created a species of dramatic composition unknown to this and I believe to any other country, which he called a pantomime; it consisted of two parts, one serious, and the other comic. By the help of gay scenes, fine habits, grand dances, appropriate music, and other decorations, he exhibited a story from Ovid's *Metamorphoses* or some other fabulous writer. Between the pauses or acts of this serious representation, he interwove a comic fable, consisting chiefly of the courtship of Harlequin and Columbine, with a variety of surprising adventures and tricks, which were produced by the magic wand of Harlequin; such as the sudden transformation of palaces and temples to huts and cottages; of men and women into wheel-barrows and joint-stools; of trees turned to houses; colonnades to beds of tulips; and mechanic shops into serpents and ostriches.[7]

Such were the genuinely dramatic *pantomimes anglaises* which the English troupes were to bring with success to the Paris fairs between 1737 and 1750.

[6] Thelma Niklaus, *Harlequin* (New York, 1956), pp. 100 ff.
[7] Thomas Davies, *Memoirs of the Life of David Garrick* (London, 1808), p. 129.

The first of the dancers, Phillips by name, was a transitional figure between the old and the new pantomime types. Already an experienced performer on trestle and stage in London, he first appeared at the Saint Laurent fair in 1737. The Paris commentators reported Phillips as sensational in a Harlequin-Columbine scene played opposite his wife, a comical drunken peasant's dance, an interpretation of a French *petit-maître*, and in several other sketches. From the roles which he presented, this actor must have been versatility itself. Phillips was also accompanied by his daughter, who played a role in the pantomime. Two months later, in August, Phillips again appeared, this time in charge of a successful pantomime bearing the promising English title, *A New Entertainment of Dancing and Singing*. This production was again varied in nature and included a number of songs in English by one of the ladies of the company.[8]

The following year saw the arrival of an English dancer and director of a troupe, Henry Delamain, who opened independently with a *pantomime anglaise* at the Saint Laurent fair. The talents of his company proved so popular that they actually drew larger crowds than the Opéra Comique. Pontou, the director of that theatre, was so impressed that he engaged Delamain's company rather than risk rivalry in the next year.[9] The English dancers, consequently, appeared at both fairs in 1739, offering, among other highly successful items, a *fête anglaise* with *divertissements*. Their pantomime in particular received the flattering description of having been "parfaitement exécutée." Unfortunately, as a result of differences with his French sponsor, Delamain disbanded his company at the close of the season at Saint Germain fair.[10]

The chief among these artists, Roberti or Roberts, had made his Paris début in 1737 at the Opéra Comique presenting a solo interlude *La Découpure*. Enthusiastically received in that role, he appeared the following year at Saint Germain in a prologue, *Le Carnaval*. Such was his popularity that he was engaged by Delamain for the season of 1739 and after the company had broken up appeared in the Saint Laurent pantomime that summer. Roberts finally achieved the ultimate triumph for a foreigner, an invitation to dance in Restier's Grande

[8]Parfait and Parfait, *Mémoires*, II, pp. 121 ff.
[9]A. Heulhard, *La Foire Saint Laurent* (Paris, 1878), p. 227.
[10]E. Campardon, *Les Spectacles de la foire* (Paris, 1877), II (under Main, de la).

Troupe Etrangère, where in 1742 he took the chief parts in both the Saint Germain productions.

Delamain's other leading pantomimist was called La Tour. After the company disbanded in 1739 La Tour joined the Restier troupe directly and for three seasons carried the Harlequin roles.[11] He also appeared in a *fête anglaise* in 1740 supported by two other Englishmen, Hendrick and Ferguson, who played minor roles with the Grande Troupe Etrangère for some years. La Tour's French name recalls that there were at this time in England numerous Huguenots whose ancestors had fled France after the revocation of the Edict of Nantes. A proportion of these entered the theatrical profession and some of them achieved a revenge by returning to France temporarily.

The season of 1745 saw the beginning of a new phenomenon. Until this time British successes had usually resulted from collaboration with the Opéra Comique, the great exception, Delamain's independent production, having been hastily absorbed by Pontou. A new situation now emerged in which the British entertainers substituted for those of the Opéra Comique.

This resulted from a significant advance in French entertainment. In 1745 the gifted author of comic opera libretti, Favart, supplied for the Saint Germain fair a work entitled *Acajou*; this, bearing the familiar title of *opéra comique*, was nevertheless really a comic opera in the modern sense: in addition to containing the familiar satirical parody of a grand opera, it was intrinsically itself a lyric opera. But, although presaging a new type, it still caricatured the singers of the Académie Royale de Musique; even the Comédiens Français were mimicked by ingenious arias in which Favart had parodied their bombastic declamation in chromatic form. The smouldering quarrel between the state troupe and their impertinent rivals flared up once more. The Académie Royale recognized the menace of the new lyric form to its own position and joined the attack. Favart bent before the blast by putting the most offensive scenes into the old *vaudeville* couplets. But despite his submission the Opéra Comique was officially suppressed and did not reopen until 1752.

Momentarily worsted, Favart none the less did not relinquish his connection with the Opéra Comique building, and to fill its vacant stage he brought in the English director of a pantomime company, Mr.

[11]D'Auriac, *Le Théâtre de la foire*, p. 47.

Mathews, who, although ostensibly managing the productions, actually worked under his French collaborator.[12] The company began by giving English works but the climax of the season was a highly successful pantomime opera *Les Vendanges de Tempé* by Favart himself.

Successful as Mr. Mathews' season had been he did not renew his arrangement with Favart; and during the Saint Germain season of 1746 the Opéra Comique premises were occupied by another English pantomime company directed by a Mrs. Sandham. Without any collaborator other than her London composer of pantomimes, Mr. Nilock, this courageous lady carried through a series of presentations including mythological extravaganzas, Harlequin adventures, and pastoral items.[13] In her last productions, she enlivened the entertainment with an exhibition of fireworks, a diversion then keenly enjoyed by the French. The pyrotechnical displays of that time included not only set pieces of both mythological and contemporary groups, but also the most ambitious rocket and illumination effects, and even mobile displays borne down the Seine in boats. A contemporary print of the *feux d'artifice* celebrating the Dauphin's marriage in 1745 leaves no doubt as to the impressive nature of these diversions.[14] Yet, although her troupe was described as the best in Paris, Mrs. Sandham appeared at Saint Germain, for only a single season.

Her failure to return was probably the result of a piece of theatrical machination. In 1746 three agents of the Académie Royale de Musique administered an English troupe in the Opéra Comique theatre under the name of Le Nouveau Spectacle Pantomime. They began by adhering to the traditional pantomime entertainment, as a report on their opening suggests: "L'Opéra Comique reopened its theatre yesterday, Wednesday, with an Italian pantomime *Ninna* presented by a new English company with introductory numbers by tightrope dancers and acrobats."[15] The group presented a full season of ballets, pantomimes, ballet-pantomimes, *divertissements*, and firework displays. Towards the middle of the season the directors took a bold step by presenting *Le Polygame*, a parody of *Amestis*, then playing at the Opéra, and *Les Talents Comiques*, a blatant caricature of another

[12]C. Parfait, *Dictionnaire des théâtres* (Paris, 1756; 7 vols.), II, p. 469. Also VI, p. 69.
[13]A. Boudet, *Les Affiches de Paris* (Paris, 1746–50; 5 vols.), I, 14 February–17 March, 1746.
[14]Paul Lacroix, *XVIIIe siècle—Institutions, usages et costumes* (Paris, 1875), pp. 380-1. A plate appears facing p. 380.
[15]Boudet, *Les Affiches de Paris*, II, June 29, 1747.

Opéra production *Les Talents Lyriques*. Then with an audacity which must indicate the approval of their official backers, the promoters changed the name of the company to that of Opéra Comique Pantomime and gradually transformed its traditional pantomimes into pantomime-operas precisely as Favart had done two years before. This combination of English and French types and talents proved so popular that the same directors continued with steady success until 1750. At that point dissatisfied Royal players managed to invoke the official ban and in June, 1750, new regulations prohibiting dialogue, singing, streamer dialogue, or explanation of the plot were rigidly enforced.

This apparently favourable opportunity for English companies offering mute ballet pantomimes was destroyed in 1752 by the official re-establishment of the Opéra Comique. The new director, Jean Louis Monnet, recently returned from London, determined to raise public taste and resolutely imposed a more dramatic form upon the operas. Abandoning the crude burlesque and the old *vaudevilles* of the fairs, he offered completely new musical compositions frequently with the charming libretti of Favart.

These improvements would have strongly challenged British competition in normal circumstances. But more potent forces were present also in the form of international tension. In Paris, the English were decidedly out of favour. In place of the once popular *fête anglais* we see Monnet in 1756 presenting *Le Mariage par Escalade* in which the lampooning of the English was so violent as to evoke protests from French Anglophils. At the same time, Monnet, who at least did admire the theatrical capacity of the English, was, by a fine irony, reaping a rich harvest at the Saint Laurent fair from an adaptation of *The Devil to Pay* presented as *Le Double Métamorphose, ou Le Diable à Quatre*. After 1755 the Seven Years' War eliminated British entertainers until the Peace of Paris in 1763.

Even before the end of the war foreign dancers and pantomimists from Holland and Italy threatened to dominate the fairs. The French response was as energetic as it was unexpected. A generation of French dancers developed, in such numbers and of such quality that they were able to carry the war into the enemy camp by visiting England. Other, even more important, factors affected the situation. In 1762, the Opéra Comique, after a highly profitable decade under Monnet and Favart, was arbitrarily merged with the royal troupe Les Italiens. The tendency in the new troupe was to diminish still further the old opera-parodies and the elements of ballet-pantomime in favour of Favart's modern lyric productions. This largely eliminated the need of foreign visitors in the Opéra Comique.

There remained the fairs, particularly Saint Germain, which had retained greater vitality than its rival. By unhappy coincidence, however, a disastrous fire reduced the entire construction of Saint Germain to ruins in the spring of 1762.[16] None the less, the buildings were rebuilt and strenuous attempts were made to revive the languishing *forain* tradition. Pantomimists from England, though rare, did not totally disappear. In 1776 a Dutch-English troupe presented a programme at Saint Germain. The title of their pantomime, *Les Ressorts Amoureux d'Harlequin*, suggests that it was completely in the old tradition. Probably with experience gained in the frost fairs of London, they also presented some remarkable acts on skates.[17] The attempts to resurrect the fairs included the founding of two new ones, those of Saint Ovide and Saint Clair, both of short duration. However, during the Saint Ovide fair a company of Spanish and English dancers and pantomimists attempted the old formula.[18] Finally, at the Saint Germain fairs of 1787 and 1788 Nicolet brought in two pantomime troupes, one Dutch, the other described as the Troupe Royale de Londres.[19] The Revolution, with its confiscation of church property, gave the death blow to the ancient fairs; and with the Restoration the last vestiges of these institutions vanished completely.

While the chief emphasis in this account has been given to the actual performers, the composers of the *pantomimes anglaises*, who contributed largely to the success of the players, should not be forgotten. Mr. Nilock, who provided scripts for Mrs. Sandham, has already been mentioned. A far more important figure was Mr. Mainbray, the author who supplied the larger proportion of the highly successful pantomimes presented by the various English companies. The curt attribution "pantomime de Mainbray de Londres" constantly appears in the *Almanachs des spectacles* during the most brilliant seasons of the English companies at the fairs. Discussing the English influence around

---

[16]P. Fromageot, *La Foire Saint Germain* (Paris, n.d.), reproduces two contemporary prints of the ruins.
[17]P. J. Nougaret, *Les Spectacles de la foire* (Paris, 1778-80; 7 vols.), I, p. 8.
[18]P. J. Nougaret, *Les Spectacles des foires* (Paris, 1774 et seq.; 2 vols.), I, pp. 146 ff.
[19]Fromageot, *La Foire Saint Germain*, p. 141.

1740, Albert writes: "M. Mainbray of London, with the collaboration of Restier in the dancing and of the painter Charmoton for the settings, offered increasingly formidable competition to the Opéra Comique with his sumptously staged pantomimes."[20] Mainbray was thoroughly versatile in the matter of subjects, treating the whole pantomime repertoire of Harlequinades, pseudo-mythological spectacles, pastorals, topical productions, and the constantly popular *fêtes anglaises*. The one uniform feature marking his contributions was the outstanding success which they enjoyed season after season. Indeed, on several occasions, mediocre operas were carried by their splendidly executed accompanying pantomimes.

The English contribution to the French theatre during the first half of the eighteenth century might, then, be described as the practical demonstration by British artists in numerous examples of a special form of entertainment, the *pantomime anglaise*. The English visits developed in the French a taste for, and some capacity in producing, pantomimes of the English type. Finally, British dancers taught their French counterparts so well by their example that the latter eventually reciprocated and invaded England.

[20] Albert, *Les Théâtres de la foire* (Paris, 1900), p. 180.

4 · "Cut the Dialect and Come to the 'Osses"

The absorption of the pantomimists of the Opéra Comique into the Italian troupe and the progressive disappearance of the fairs not only eliminated most of the foreign performers but also left their public at a loss for entertainment. Varied and costly attempts were made by the Parisian directors to satisfy it. Their most outstanding offerings were inspired by English models and called by the same names. Between 1764 and the Revolution, three establishments called *Waux-hall* were exploited with varying fortunes. All were patterned on London's Vauxhall and Ranelagh Gardens, two places of diversion which had enjoyed high favour since the 1730's as fashionable resorts for tea, entertainment, and conversation. From Hogarth's depictions of them, the so-called gardens depended chiefly for their popularity upon the splendour of their appointments, lighting, and other visual effects. The earliest Parisian version was a genuinely international phenomenon inspired by England and engineered by the Italian pyrotechnician, Torre, who in 1764 founded the *Waux-hall de Torre*, as the Parisians called it.[1] It consisted of an immense theatre building in which pyrotechnical pantomimes were presented. *The Forge of Vulcan* and *Eurydice in the Underworld*, both given in 1766, particularly delighted the patrons. Unfortunately, the protests of alarmed householders in the vicinity resulted in the closing of this type of production. In 1768 Torre opened a new spectacle more closely patterned on the London version. Under the reminiscent title of *Les Fêtes foraines*, it offered brilliant decorations and lighting, vocal and instrumental concerts, games of chance and skill, and even brief *scènes de parade* by first-class actors.[2] The success of this venture was halted by yet another intervention of monopoly.

[1] Louis Petit de Bachaumont, *Mémoires Secrets*, édités par Maisrobert et Mouffle d'Angesville (Paris, 1777 et. seq.; 31 vols.), I, p. 305.
[2] E. Campardon, *Les Spectacles de la foire* (Paris, 1877; 2 vols.), II (under Waux-hall).

In 1771 two former directors of the Opéra Comique decided to enter the same field as Torre, and obtained a monopoly of such entertainment. However, in spite of singers, pantomimes, the ever-popular fireworks, and even a troupe of English equestrians, the Colysée, as it was called, languished to a close in 1779.

A *Waux-hall d'hiver* also appeared at the Saint Germain fair in 1769. It carried on successfully until, in 1785, the management moved it nearer to its rival, the Palais Royal, where it specialized in concerts, balls, and pyrotechnic displays. The third *Waux-hall*, showing little originality and handicapped by an inaccessible location, never gained public favour.

The popular entertainers of Paris had apparently not produced any fully satisfactory substitute for the old productions of the fairs. Moreover, in the middle eighties, the hectic pleasures of the Palais Royal, really a gaming establishment, injured other places of popular entertainment in somewhat the same way as the gambling mania which raged around 1720 injured the theatres and fairs of that day. Once again, as in the case of the pantomimes, English entertainers provided a successful form of entertainment. The new feature was the equestrian spectacle.

A prominent element in English-French exchanges of the eighteenth century was the importation of pure-blooded English horses for carriage and riding purposes. We encounter, for example, at the Saint Germain fair an Englishman Kuensly (probably a French mis-spelling) who in 1709 and 1710 displayed wonderful horses and on occasion was prepared to sell them.[3] It is not clear whether these were performing animals or simply saleable beasts. In any case, the French became increasingly fond of English horses as the century advanced. Riding, and particularly racing, often with ruinous betting involved, became a habit of the gentleman, and the mark particularly of the snob.

Later in the century horse-racing had still a tremendous popularity and a large number of the horses were still being imported from the British Isles. At the Newmarket français, opened in 1775, the Queen herself deigned to meet the English jockeys after the races. This popularity was no passing fad. A considerable English establishment was maintained at Chantilly in connection with the race tracks there; indeed, this unique English colony (complete even to a Methodist

[3] P. Fromageot, *La Foire Saint Germain* (Paris, n.d.), p. 36.

church) was definitively closed only after the Second World War. In eighteenth-century Paris, however, the outstanding development in the equestrian field was the introduction of performing horses into pantomime spectacles. The Italian impresario Franconi had a part in this activity, but the dominant role was played by four British equestrians.

One of the leading attractions at the Colysée in 1774 was a Sieur Hyam, as the bills called him. Mr. Hyam, under the description of *Ecuyer Anglais*, presented a programme which included the exhibition of his trained horses in various manoeuvres, followed by a display of his own and his assistants' skill.[4] Hyam was an amazingly good rider to judge from the circumstantial and enthusiastic accounts left by observers. He excelled in all the usual exercises of the equestrian acrobat, riding in a standing position on one and also two horses, leaping from a galloping mount to alight on a following animal, and diving through hoops from a galloping horse. His most thrilling feat involved hanging at apparently impossible angles from fast-travelling horses to snatch objects from the ground or to place rings with incredible precision on appropriate projections. Similarly talented, his feminine star Miss Mason also performed with exceptional skill on both one and two horses. Hyam even carried in his troupe two juveniles, boy and girl, aged five and eight, both of whom impressed the crowd, as indeed did the horses themselves in their special numbers. There is no doubt as to Hyam's warm reception in 1774; in the next year he again presented his performances throughout the summer season, first at the Ruggieri hall, a lesser rival of the various "*Waux-halls*," then, towards the end of the season, in the gardens of Armand's café on the Boulevard du Temple.

At Armand's, Hyam and his troupe were described as surpassing themselves with a more elaborate programme, which included a good deal of comedy. Here is the first suggestion of English clowns, who were later to enjoy such popularity in France. Mrs. Hyam also appeared in what was a novelty for Paris; her balancing act on the *fil d'archal* or high-wire. We are inclined to believe that the juveniles already referred to were Mr. Hyam's own children for we read that at the end of September he left with his entire family to continue his triumphs at

[4] De Bachaumont, *Mémoires Secrets*, VII, p. 231.

Lyons.[5] In his publicity Mr. Hyam modestly titled himself *Le Héros Anglais*; there seems little doubt that his French admirers were quite ready to accept his description.

Somewhat less successful was a similar presentation in 1778 under the direction of Jacob Bates. This equestrian (whom the French disguise in all their references as Beates) installed himself on the Champs Elysées, in the neighbourhood of the Colysée, and gave the regular programme of his class. Apparently one season sufficed him, for his troupe is not heard of again. An interesting handbill describes Bates in English as "the famous English horse rider" and depicts him in heroic posture beside his horse while, in the background, members of his company are engaged in various exercises before an open air audience. The tri-lingual text of the poster suggests that he may have tried his fortunes in Germany as well as in France.[6]

Eclipsing all his predecessors in the length of his sojourn, the ambitious nature of his productions, and in his effect on French popular entertainment, Philip Astley first became prominent in Paris in 1782. The career of this extraordinary man exemplifies rough versatility and courageous determination in the face of multiple and varied reverses. Astley joined the English cavalry as a young man and became a horse-breaker and trainer. After distinguished battle service, he retired from army life to give exhibitions of horsemanship. In 1774 he made a visit to Paris in the troupe of Razade, an equestrian in the service of the king of Sardinia. This brief and not particularly notable interlude concluded, he returned to England. After varied success in the English provinces, he set up a circus in London for equestrian displays. In the next year, 1782, he again made his appearance in Paris and there established a most ambitious amphitheatre near the Faubourg du Temple. On his elaborate posters the establishment bore the title of Amphithéâtre Anglais. The equestrian elements were always dominant for Astley loved horses, but there were many others. The high-wire on which Mrs. Hyam had pleased the crowds in 1775 was the means of displaying the virtuosity of an acrobat clown, Saunders (or Sanders), whom Astley had specially brought from the Royal Theatre in London, and who received the honour of very large type on the bills as well as

[5] P. J. Nougaret, *Les Spectacles des foires* (Paris, 1774 *et. seq.*; 2 vols.) I, pp. 84 ff.
[6] Baron de Vaux, *Ecuyers et écuyères* (Paris, 1893), plate facing p. 296.

very cordial receptions from the audiences.⁷ The constant popularity of fireworks was recognized by elaborate pyrotechnic displays, often in close relation to other parts of the programme. Clowns, such as those in Hyam's troupe, were just beginning to be appreciated in France; Astley's clowns were of the best. Finally, a large orchestra furnished a spirited setting for the whole production.⁸

These programmes included plays of the melodramatic pantomime variety in which, as might be expected, fine horsemanship played a prominent role. The plays can justifiably be related to the spectacular pantomimes in which Astley's compatriots had gained favour at the earlier fairs, although Astley's productions were considerably more grandiose. The company made no pretence of presenting anything other than popular entertainment. "The drama of Astley's Amphitheatre," writes an English commentator, who enjoyed attending it as a boy, "was always peculiar to itself; its most salient features were noise, blood, thunder and gunpowder; tyrant kings and savage chiefs of the most ferocious types of theatrical humanity, and heroes of the most impossible bravery and virtue. Every great battle . . . has probably been at some time depicted upon that stage."⁹

Astley, a superb horseman, regularly took a leading role in his Parisian productions, accompanied from the beginning by his son John, then only seventeen years of age but already an accomplished and attractive equestrian. Mrs. Astley also appeared in the ring with her husband, while Lucy Saunders, a daughter of the leading comic performer already mentioned, frequently played opposite the son. One of the most popular performances given by the father and son was a type of musical ride. "The Astley's," writes Nougaret, "carried out with infinite grace a minuet on horseback which consisted of the steps known as full speed, pirouette and stamp."¹⁰ This item, in which the horses were travelling at full gallop at times, was called the Devonshire Minuet and drew the admiration even of the great dancer Vestris. Horace Walpole also wrote enthusiastically of the Astley presentations:

⁷Georges Cain, *Les Anciens Théâtres de Paris* (Paris, 1906). A facsimile of an Astley bill appears on p. 47.
⁸P. J. Nougaret, *Les Spectacles de la foire* (Paris, 1778–80; 7 vols.), I, pp. 206 ff; II, p. 150.
⁹H. Barton Baker, *The London Stage: Its History and Traditions from 1576 to 1888* (London, 1889; 2 vols.), II, p. 226.
¹⁰P. J. Nougaret, *Histoire des chevaux célèbres* (Paris, 1810), p. 255.

But though Mercury did not tread the air with more sovereign agility than the son, it was the father I contemplated with most admiration! What a being, who dared to conceive that he could make horses dance ... and that men, women, and children might be trained to possess themselves on, over, round the rapidity of two, three, four race-horses, and neither tremble for their necks, nor forget one attitude that is becoming.[11]

John Astley's handsome appearance won him special favour with the ladies, including Marie Antoinette who, after one of his performances, presented him with a diamond-studded gold medal. Her Majesty also hailed the young favourite as the English Rose, a flattering comparison with Vestris, then known as the French Rose. As well, the King, after a command performance directed by the young man at Versailles in April, 1786, rewarded him with the gift of a hundred louis.[12]

The Paris Amphitheatre carried on successfully and, when it moved in 1786, enlarged and redecorated its establishment to the satisfaction of the Parisians. One production, characteristically entitled *Le Fougueux Coursier*, earned the substantial sum of 325,000 francs. In 1784, a year of much suffering in France because of the severe cold, Nicolet, the director of the Grands Danseurs du Roi, conceived the idea of giving benefit performances for the poor. The practice continued, and Astley's benefit programme of 1785 raised an enormous sum.[13]

Frequently a presentation which had proved popular in Astley's London establishment was transported to Paris. In a letter to the Earl of Strafford, September 12, 1783, Horace Walpole notes that, in a dearth of entertainment, he had resorted to visiting Astley's and had been considerably impressed. "But," he continued, "I shall not have even Astley's now; Her Majesty the Queen of France ... has sent for the whole of the *dramatis personae*."[14] Occasionally the process was reversed. In 1788 an entirely new pantomime was given at the London Amphitheatre under the title of *The Humours of Gil Blas*; the production was advertised as having been performed with applause in Paris.

The Revolution was a severe blow to Astley's Paris fortunes. Absent from France at the outbreak of the political disturbances, he asked Mme Laurent, the mother of one of his London acrobats to continue the performances at the Paris establishment in order to avoid its

[11]Peter Cunningham, ed., *The Letters of Horace Walpole, Fourth Earl of Orford* (Edinburgh, 1906), VIII, p. 407.
[12]Nougaret, *Les Spectacles de la foire*, II, p. 152.
[13]*Ibid.*, I. p. 26.
[14]Cunningham, ed., *The Letters of Horace Walpole, Fourth Earl of Orford*, VIII, p. 408.

confiscation by the government. When the European coalition declared war, the old cavalry veteran rejoined the British army. His amphitheatre, left vacant in March, 1791, was rented by a group of young actors who styled themselves Les Petits Comédiens. Since all theatrical monopoly had been abolished, they intended to appear as Le Théâtre des Comédiens sans Titre. Unfortunately, after only a three-day run, the word *Relâche* made a permanent appearance on their doors.[15]

In 1793, Franconi, an Italian competitor of Astley, found his establishment at Lyons burned by the Republican invaders. He rented the Astley Amphitheatre, changed the name to the Cirque Olympique, and began by presenting grandiose patriotic spectacles. Franconi could well feel at home in Astley's. From 1783 he had been associated with his English rival and on different occasions had presented his Lyons company in Astley's Paris Amphitheatre while the English company was on provincial tours in France during the summer. Franconi's patriotic *grands spectacles* of 1793 were favourably received in Paris, but he was not to enjoy his privilege of exploitation for long. The government, requiring the building for use as a barracks, requisitioned it until the close of hostilities in 1802.

With the Peace of Amiens, Astley returned to Paris and, dealing directly with Bonaparte himself, he not only gained possession of his property but even received rent for its occupation by French troops. Unfortunately he had to withdraw almost immediately and with some difficulty from France, owing to a decree ordering the detention of all British subjects. In 1814 he hastened back to Paris but, before he had the time to implement any further plans, he died and was buried in that city. His son, the idol of the Paris crowds in the eighties, succeeded briefly to the management of the English establishments, relinquished them in 1817, and in 1821 died in Paris, a relatively young man.

Andrew Ducrow, the man who really carried on the Astley tradition, has been termed the greatest of all equestrian artists and the most perfect of pantomimists. "The glory of Ducrow," wrote an admiring contemporary, "lies in his poetical impersonations. Why the horse is but the air, as it were, on which he flies."[16] The son of a Belgian

[15]L. Péricaud, *Le Théâtre des petits comédiens de S. A. S. Monseigneur le comte de Beaujolais* (Paris, 1909), p. 121.
[16]Christopher North, *Noctes Ambrosianae*, as cited by H. Barton Baker, *The London Stage: Its History and Traditions from 1576 to 1888*, II, p. 223.

strong man in Astley's London Amphitheatre, young Ducrow from his earliest years began a rigorous apprenticeship in all the arts of the pantomimist's profession. He quickly developed superb skill and particularly the courage and boldness which made him popular with audiences in later years. At fifteen he was already chief equestrian at Astley's in London, and in 1813 made his début as a pantomimist with equally great success. His chief triumphs were really achieved by a combination of the two forms of entertainment: Ducrow literally became an actor on horseback.

In 1814, Ducrow joined the Cirque Olympique of the celebrated impresario Blondell and, accompanied by several members of his family, began a continental tour with an appearance in Belgium. Enormously successful visits to the chief cities of the French provinces followed. The culmination occurred at Lyons, where, in young Astley's pattern, he received a gold medal from the hands of a royal lady, the Duchesse d'Angoulême. Naturally, Franconi's managers did not fail to notice this remarkable young equestrian, especially when they found all their younger performers imitating his methods and acts. Long negotiations took place, in the course of which Franconi displayed his determination to enlist the English artist by offering him all the profits exceeding three hundred francs a performance. Finally, in December, 1818, Ducrow's début at the Franconi Cirque Olympique introduced a triumphal run as an equestrian and later as a pantomimist. Ducrow first presented at Franconi's the special type of equestrian pageant which they termed an *entrée*. He also initiated several particularly daring double riding acts in which he would carry a second performer on his shoulders while standing up on one or two fast-running horses. In such acts as *Cupid and Zephyr* and *Little Red Riding Hood* he was accompanied by his sister, then barely more than a child. In still another distinctive specialty he presented what he styled *poses plastiques*, which really consisted of elegant *tableaux vivants* of classical inspiration, all executed on horseback.[17]

In the spring of 1819 the idol of Paris, as he was called, returned to England to recruit a number of English pantomimists and clowns. With these reinforcements, including his brother John, who performed as a clown, and his sister, who later achieved fame on the legitimate stage as Mrs. Broadfoot, he led an elaborate combined dramatic and

[17]Thos. Frost, *Circus Life and Circus Celebrities* (London, 1875), p. 55.

equestrian production across the south of France throughout the summer season. His chief attraction was a melodramatic equestrian pantomime entitled *The Magic Tomb*. This performance combined the mysterious, the spectacular, and the comic in proportions which proved highly satisfying to French audiences. Occasional difficulties arose from native competition. Faced at one point with the determined rivalry of a French competitor, who had enlisted the services of the French comedian Mazurier, Ducrow daringly promised to duplicate on horseback whatever Mazurier did on foot. This rather reckless commitment was duly executed, to the great pleasure of the public.

Becoming manager of Astley's London Amphitheatre late in 1819, Ducrow spent the rest of his career directing productions in England. The word "poetical," quoted earlier, is one which Ducrow would probably have shuddered to hear applied to his person or his work. Having received but little formal education, he remained all but illiterate and refused to take any but the briefest of speaking parts. His particular skill was as a producer and it lay in his indisputable genius for grouping, for massing harmonious colours, and for organizing vigorous and convincing action. A purveyor of *grands spectacles*, he held more literary elements in profound contempt, and, always seeking to emphasize the spectacular, strove in his own productions to reduce them to the minimum required for the exposition. His favourite stage direction was typical: "Cut the dialect [dialogue] and come to the 'osses." Essentially a man of vigorous and dramatic action, known as the king of mimes and the colossus of equestrians, this consummate artist left his mark not only on the equestrian spectacle in general, but also on that of France in particular.

Astley's Amphithéâtre Anglais came into the hands of the Franconis after the death of Philip Astley in 1814 and was once again named the Cirque Olympique. The Franconis renovated and moved the establishment repeatedly, taking advantage of one of the changes to add a small theatre for the presentation of the familiar pantomime spectacles. It is interesting that one very notable artist entered the regular Paris theatres through this addition. In this theatre Frédéric Lemaître made his début before the Parisian public in 1817, and remained there until his move to the Odéon in 1820, which opened the way to his later celebrity. The pantomimes in which the future creator of the famous character Robert Macaire played the leading roles were described as *pantomimes dialoguées*. Among these pantomimes, presented in the best Astley tradition, were *Macbeth* and *Othello*, very freely adapted from the original and abundantly augmented with noise and violence. To judge from the contemporary comments upon it, the literary fare offered by the Franconi theatre never reached a very high standard. The *Revue et chronique parisienne* for 1817 commented drily that "the intelligence of the four footed actors ... which stands in strong contrast to the instinct of the bipeds will long attract the populace in search of wonders."[18] A similar squib appeared in Harel's whimsical dictionary of the theatre of 1835 to the effect that, of the two troupes, quadruped and biped, directed by the famous brothers, the four-footed artists were doing them the most credit.[19]

In their true field, that of the equestrian spectacle, the Franconi brothers did not hesitate to call upon English talent when it became available after 1815. Ducrow has already been mentioned in this connection. In 1817 an equestrian artist, Mr. Davis, made a much advertised and highly successful début on a beautifully trained animal. This gentleman was probably the same Davis who replaced young Astley as manager of the London Amphitheatre that year. During his entire month's engagement he was received "avec beaucoup d'applaudissements."[20] Again, in 1827, for the grand opening of their reconstructed Paris Amphithéâtre, the Franconis imported a group of English equestrians whom they billed as *Les Anglais au Manège*. The act appeared at intervals throughout the winter without, however, creating any notable sensation. To be outstanding against the competition at Franconi's in that period was genuinely difficult.[21]

In the same way as the French dancers of the eighteenth century turned the tables on the English artists, so, in the circus pantomime, did the French return the original English compliment with interest. It is amusing to read the anguished reactions of an English amateur of the theatre as he saw M. Martin, the celebrated lion tamer from Franconi's, putting a fair-sized menagerie through its paces on the stage of Drury Lane Theatre in 1831. "Had they gone to Astley's," he writes, "their appearance would have been hailed with delight."[22]

[18]*Revue et chronique parisienne* (Paris, 1818), I, p. 14.
[19]J. B. Harel, *Dictionnaire des théâtres* (Paris, 1836), under Cirque Olympique.
[20]*Almanach des spectacles de K.Y.Z.*, Paris, 1819, under Cirque Olympique.
[21]*Le Courrier des théâtres*, Paris, 1827–8 passim.
[22]W. P. Lennox, *Plays, Players and Playhouses* (London, 1881; 2 vols.), I, p. 177.

When shortly afterwards it was proposed that the Franconi equestrian troupe should appear at the same theatre, public opinion forced the project to be abandoned. However, another and more successful plan was fulfilled in 1848, when the Cirque National company from Paris not only played in London but played on the stage of Drury Lane.

The French readily recognized Astley's special place as the originator of equestrian entertainment in Paris, and in his discussion of the Cirque Olympique in 1838, Brazier remarked: "Franconi's circus existed long before the Directory; some years before the Revolution, an Englishman named Astley had imported that type of spectacle into France."[23]

[23] N. Brazier, *Histoire des petits théâtres* (Paris, 1838; 2 vols.), I, p. 149.

5 · The Pleasures of a Year and the Follies of a Day

Among the many private English visitors to France during the eighteenth century were the usual proportion of actors, with a variety of reasons for their visits. In general, these reasons fall into two categories: financial or personal difficulties, or a search for inspiration from the observation of French plays and players.

Cardell Goodman well illustrates the first group. Though little more than a rakehell spendthrift, he appeared successfully in London between 1677 and 1688, in spite of various broils with his fellow actors. Finally, he became involved in the Jacobite plot and fled to France, where he died two years later. Another theatrical gentleman in distress, Owen McSwinney, fled to Paris in 1710 to avoid the unpleasant results of a poor season. He must have found life there agreeable because he spent the next twenty years in France and Italy, adapting Molière's *Amour Médecin* for English presentation as *The Quack*. Theo. Cibber, also a fugitive from his creditors, took refuge in France for a brief period in 1738. In 1774 William Smith, who enjoyed the somewhat inexpilcable sobriquet of "Gentleman Smith," departed for Paris in company with Mrs. Hartley, his Lady Macbeth; his flight was only a short one and he returned to a reconciliation with his wife. Mrs. Robinson, the famous Perdita of the period, utilized the pension granted her by Fox after her liaison with the future George IV, to go to Paris in 1783. There she entered society, even to the extent of receiving kindly attention from Marie Antoinette.

More significant are the visits of certain actors who went to France to gain inspiration from the French theatre. Colley Cibber made two such journeys to study the *petit-maître* roles in which he specialized as Lord Foppington, and also to observe the methods of the celebrated actor, Baron. In 1751 Mrs. Cibber, while in Paris to recruit dancers for Rich, the pantomimist, spent her leisure time attending the theatres.

On her return she adapted one of the plays which she had especially appreciated, presenting it in March, 1752, under the title of *The Oracle*. A more modest figure, Robert Baddely, after serving as general factotum for the actor Samuel Foote, spent three years on the Continent as a valet. In the process he acquired a smattering of foreign languages and customs, which apparently served him well after his return, since his contemporary, Michael Kelly, the actor and composer, describes him as having been a creditable actor in Jewish and French roles.

David Garrick, the great theatrical figure of the century, visited France on two occasions.[1] (It is interesting to note that Garrick's paternal grandfather, La Garrique, had fled from France as a Huguenot refugee.) In the summer of 1751 the famous actor and his wife took a delayed honeymoon trip to Paris. His reputation at that time was not sufficient to command a widespread reception, yet the journey was not without both honours and excitement. For the former, the young foreign actor is said to have received the distinction of a presentation to the king. The excitement was highly melodramatic if we accept a moderately authenticated anecdote related by his biographer Fitzgerald. An English acquaintance of Garrick's was found dead after a shooting party in the *Forêt de Bondy*, and Garrick pressed the search until suspicion fell on an Italian count in the party. He had the count brought to the dead man's hotel room, and there the Italian saw the man whom he had murdered lying on the bed before him and heard his accusing voice. Thrown into confusion, he confessed his crime, quite unaware that the accuser was really Garrick displaying his exceptional powers of impersonation. Unfortunately, Garrick's journal, which might have settled debate on the authenticity of the story, has been lost.

Professionally, Garrick took advantage of his visit in various ways. With the aid of a French dancer, Devisse, he made some unsuccessful attempts to recruit dancers. He saw the young Clairon act and predicted a notable future for her. He met Favart, whose position as composer and director was by then well established. His friendship with Monnet, one of the leading theatre managers of Paris, was lengthy and cordial and when Monnet came to England shortly after, Garrick gave him good advice (which the Frenchman was not always wise

---

[1] Those wishing an exhaustive treatment of Garrick's visits to France are referred to F. A. Hedgcock, *Garrick et ses amis français* (Paris, 1911).

enough to follow), and even gave a benefit performance for him which raised over a hundred guineas.

We find further mention of Garrick's visit in the copious *Journal* of Charles Collé. Under date of July 16, 1751, M. Collé wrote:

> I dined yesterday ... with Garrick. He played for us a scene from a Shakespearean tragedy in which we easily saw that the man justly enjoys his great reputation. He sketched for us the scene in which Macbeth imagines that he sees a dagger in the air leading him to the room where he is to murder the king. He inspired terror in us; it would be impossible to depict a situation more strikingly, to render it with more fire, and at the same time to be more in command of oneself.... What he gave us was a sort of tragic pantomime, and, judging from the one example, I can unhesitatingly say that the actor is an excellent artist.[2]

Garrick's second visit took place at the time of his temporary retirement from the stage from 1763 to 1765. Arriving in Paris late in September, 1763, after the usual harrassments of eighteenth-century travel, he was delayed at the gates of Paris by an accident to the coach. The breakdown turned out to be simply a pretext arranged by the Comédiens Français, who had prepared a welcome at a near-by inn. This was but the beginning of a constant round of entertainment for Garrick. He arrived at a moment of Anglomania in literature, and at once became the honoured guest of D'Holbach and Helvétius, exchanging ideas with Diderot and Grimm, the Abbé Morellet, and a host of others. The night after his arrival he attended the Comédie Française, where Mlle Dumesnil was playing in Nivelle de la Chaussée's *Gouvernante*. He found her acting highly artificial, indeed almost a caricature of nature, but apparently he did not express this opinion to the Comédiens, for they continued to do him every honour, including that of permission to occupy the royal box when it was free. Soon after arriving he had a long conversation with Mlle Clairon, the great rival of Mlle Dumesnil. Their acquaintance dated from his first visit, and Clairon enthusiastically associated herself with the great English actor. It was rumoured that she had taken lessons from him in preparation for the production of a new play, *Blanche et Guiscard*. This whole production really formed a tribute to Garrick and great pains were taken with settings, costumes, and interpretation. The play was adapted from Thomson's *Tancred and Sigismunde*, and the opening night developed into a grand ovation to the guest of honour. Unfor-

[2]Charles Collé, *Journal et mémoires* (Paris, 1868; 3 vols.), III, p. 332.

tunately, the French version collapsed after three evenings, with Mlle Clairon's performances causing much debate.[3]

A little later what must have been a remarkable evening diversion given by the two artists took place at an English gentleman's home. First, Mlle Clairon gave a passage from *Athalie* in the hope that Garrick would perform also. He did, and for his share gave a whole series of pantomimed sketches: the dagger scene from *Macbeth*, Lear's curse, the actions of a man who had accidentally let his child fall from a window, and even a mime of a cook's boy who has dropped his tray of tarts on the ground.

Garrick encountered two other French friends in Paris, M. and Mme Suard. Mme Suard he had already met during his 1751 visit, while M. Suard, the eminent translator of Hume and Robertson, had seen him act in London and by enthusiastic reports had prepared the Paris salons for his coming. After Garrick's arrival this gentleman exerted himself to entertain his English idol and interpret him to the salons. One point which seemed to puzzle the Parisians was that the English apparently held Garrick in almost higher esteem than they did Shakespeare. According to M. Suard, this was because Garrick, having absorbed the very genius of Shakespeare, had made the great dramatist more fully comprehensible to the English public and so had won their admiration and gratitude.

After a crowded three weeks, the fêted guest continued his journey to Italy. On the way he communicated with Voltaire but, unfortunately, neither then nor on his return was he able to visit the sage of Ferney to receive enlightenment on the true merits of Shakespeare. Following the lengthy Italian interlude, which unfortunately included not only much pleasure, both as a tourist and socially, but also a severe bout of wasting illness, Garrick returned to Paris in October, 1764.

His temporary emaciation and weakness soon vanished and he once more plunged into the round of entertainments and honours. With Marmontel and De la Place, Marivaux and D'Holbach, he laid the foundations of lasting friendships, and indeed helped to set the tradition of the "agreeable Englishman" which held in Paris for many years. He aided Beaumarchais with minor phases of *Le Barbier de Seville*; he renewed his acquaintance with Monnet; even the archvillain of Shakespeare translators, Letourneur, had a word with Garrick

---

[3]Baron de Grimm, *Correspondance littéraire* (Paris, 1813), Part I, vol. III, p. 511.

about the versions of the plays which he was contemplating. And, of course, Garrick's private performances continued. Most of them were given in crowded salons, with only the merest hint of costuming, and they were accompanied by the running translations of his friend Suard to aid those who could not follow. One gathers these must have seemed needless, so vivid was Garrick's pantomime. The rigorous study and meticulous preparation apparent in everything he presented, pleased the more serious among his audiences, who saw a resemblance to the scrupulous interpretations of their idol Lekain. Grimm, for example, wrote of him: "He has perfected his talents by a profound study of nature and by researches marked by insight and sublimity."[4]

One evening the salon took up the question of imitation and originality. This was, as Diderot's writings reveal, a debate which arose frequently in French salons of that day. After Condillac had given his arguments in favour of imitation, Garrick found himself challenged for an opinion. Striking a theatrical posture, the Englishman quoted the French saying "Non, n'imitons personne et servons tous d'exemple." As one would expect, his graceful handling of the situation occasioned general admiration.

Garrick won his popularity with the partisans of rigorous preparation of roles by furnishing them with the perfect example of what they preached about naturalness and realism. The case of Diderot is especially interesting. This passionate Romantic had earlier supported the school of extemporary acting, but Garrick's extraordinary capacities forced him to change his opinion. And in 1770 his review of the pamphlet by the obscure actor Antonio Sticoti, entitled *Garrick or the English Actors*, developed into the famous *Paradoxe sur le comédien* in which Diderot completely supported Garrick's method. "Garrick," he wrote, "shows his face through a doorway and within two seconds I see his countenance pass swiftly from extreme joy to astonishment from astonishment to sadness from sadness to dejection from dejection to despair and then revert with the same rapidity from where he has arrived to where he began."[5] Diderot contends that Garrick could not possibly have felt all these emotions, but had produced the impression of them by studied art. Grimm, on the other hand, admired the absorption of the actor in his role. "The chief art of David Garrick,"

[4] *Ibid.*, IV, p. 502.
[5] Denis Diderot, *Oeuvres complètes* (Paris, 1875), VIII, p. 352.

he wrote, "lies in the ease which he displays ... in putting himself into the situation of the character which he is to represent: and when he has once really grasped the role, he ceases to be Garrick, and becomes the character which he has assumed."[6]

The one dour face appears to have been that of M. Collé. His account of a disastrous dinner at which he strove to entertain Garrick (and, of course, to be entertained by him) is a rare mixture of the grotesque and the pathetic. Collé had apparently striven by every possible means to insinuate himself into Garrick's good graces, and the unwillingness of the great actor to respond put the host in very bad humour. When the discomfited Collé approached Garrick the following day with a further invitation he received a rather blunt refusal, given, as the irate dramatist put it, "with English impertinence, by which I mean with the utmost vulgarity." And the ruffled gentleman fumes through another page of abuse directed against Garrick, his writings, his profession and his race, all of which come under heavy judgment.

Elsewhere, however, all was cordiality and admiration. The men of the Comédie Française entertained him repeatedly and, unlike the disgruntled Collé, were rewarded with a long series of imitations. His celebrated exploit when, with Préville, he deluded the whole village of Passy into believing him utterly intoxicated remains an amusing anecdote of his skill as a pantomimist.[7] As might be expected, the question of his appearing on the French stage was raised by his friends of the royal troupe. But, although he understood French very well, Garrick did not feel capable of going before the public with his *confrères* of the Théâtre Française. He did, however, cherish a hope which was to be fulfilled after his death. As Garat informs us: "Another of Garrick's hopes ... was that France and England from time to time should send each other their best troupes and that we might see French drama in London and English drama in Paris."[8]

In spite of all this Garrick's heart was still with the London stage, and in mid-April, 1765, he left Paris to try his fortunes with the fickle London public, a public which he feared might, instead of demanding his return, simply forget him. As he was leaving Paris a

[6] Grimm, *Correspondance littéraire*, Part I, vol. IV, p. 500.
[7] *Ibid.*, pp. 502–3.
[8] D. G. Garat, *Mémoires historiques du XVIIIe siècle* (Paris, 1821; 2 vols.), II, pp. 124 ff., gives various interesting details on Garrick.

tempest-in-a-teapot battle broke out between the Comédiens Français and the government as certain of the leading members of the royal troupe had refused to perform when especially requested to do so by the government. The rebellious players, led by Clairon, soon found themselves in prison, and from there Lekain, Molé, and Mlle Clairon wrote to their English friend. His reply was prompt, his offers of help generous. Long after the theatrical flurry had passed over, these fellow-players, and a great many of the *élite* of Paris, recalled with affectionate respect the unique personality which had moved among them.

The pleasure and profit were not all on one side. Garrick returned to England restored in health and spirits and from this time forward a new Garrick appeared in London. After dallying still further with the notion of complete retirement, he acceded to his sovereign's request and opened to a packed house which included His Majesty. His playing revealed a new grace and elegance, almost certainly derived from the salons of Paris; his whole bearing displayed greater poise. Garrick the stage manager profited greatly also, for he brought back with him a large number of ideas about the furnishing and ordering of the stage itself.

Garrick wielded an influence much wider than the merely social or personal. One cannot be dogmatic in a matter of an individual's influence, but in such fields as his it is usually a few outstanding figures who guide a general movement. Hughes has said of Garrick: "His influence extended far beyond the confines of his own country and may be traced throughout the theatre of all Europe."[9] With this we may perhaps connect a more general description of Nicoll's:

If we cast our gaze over Europe in the eighteenth century we can see that everywhere it was the Elizabethan drama which inspired the rising theatres of the continent and drove back the chilling theories of neo-classical France, until in time France itself gave way and in Victor Hugo produced a romantic and bizarre genius akin to Shakespeare himself.[10]

From the seventeenth century forward England and France influenced each other considerably by the mutual adaptation of plays. These adaptations were usually of French plays into English, often rather clumsily done by literary hacks. Of all those who imported French plays into England during the eighteenth century, Thomas

[9] Glenn Hughes, *The Story of the Theatre* (New York, 1928), p. 198.
[10] Allardyce Nicoll, *British Drama* (New York, 1933), p. 214.

Holcroft was certainly the most remarkable. He is interesting for two reasons: his other contacts of a literary and dramatic nature in France, and the extraordinary method of his most noted adaptation.

Born in 1745, after a childhood and youth of privation, this actor of all work finally gained a precarious foothold with Macklin's company and that of the Kembles. Holcroft exerted himself in a great variety of theatrical activities, acting both principal characters and old men, playing the violin and supplying new plays. In 1775 he sent a letter of application to Garrick which prophetically outlined his talents: he claimed to know "something of French and fencing" and also stated that he had "a very quick memory as I can repeat any part under four lengths at six hours notice."[11] Garrick remained unimpressed by these gifts, and Holcroft continued to cling desperately to the fringes of the theatrical world as a minor actor, a musician, and, increasingly, as an author of plays, both original and adapted.

Finally, in 1783, Holcroft determined to attempt a career in Paris as correspondent and translator. He crossed the Channel armed with several letters of introduction, an engagement with a London paper to contribute paragraphs of topical interest on the Paris scene, and an agreement with a publisher, John Rivington, to furnish regular information regarding new works suitable for translation. Holcroft soon began to work on several of these, particularly the writings of Mme de Genlis, with whom he later enjoyed both frequent correspondence and personal acquaintance. He met also a fellow translator, M. Bonneville, whose work, however, lay more with German material.

By various expedients the visitor managed to gain entry to the salons of several French noblemen. At the home of the Duc de Chartres he read a number of scenes from Shakespeare before a brilliant assembly and apparently pleased everyone thoroughly. With the Comte de Catelan, an avowed admirer of Shakespeare, he engaged in a friendly debate both by word of mouth and by letter. As was inevitable, they discussed the question of the English playwright in relation to the French dramatic poets; in this exchange Voltaire, France's severest critic of Shakespeare, naturally came in for stern condemnation. Unfortunately, Holcroft's remittances from England arrived at increasingly long intervals; at last, in October, weary of fruitless waiting

---

[11]W. Hazlitt, *Complete Works of Wm. Hazlitt*, ed. P. P. Howe (London, 1933; 15 vols.), III, p. 73.

and of humiliating dependence on Bonneville, the would-be foreign correspondent returned to England.

In the following year, the news of the overwhelming success being achieved by Beaumarchais' *Le Mariage de Figaro* fired Holcroft to attempt the most singular of his many exploits. He determined to obtain a copy of the play, adapt it for English presentation, and sell it to a London theatre. In Paris, however, he discovered to his chagrin not only that printed copies were unobtainable but also that even the actors' manuscripts were jealously guarded.[12] Undismayed, Holcroft sought the aid of his friend Bonneville. Attending the play night after night, the two memorized at high tension, taking such brief notes as they dared, and then rushed home to write down the scenes, comparing versions and noting doubtful points to be verified the next night. When, after ten days, they had a version which satisfied them, Holcroft hastened back to London, there to begin the translation and adaptation of the pilfered masterpiece.

Shortly before Christmas, Harris of Covent Garden brought out the play under the title, *The Follies of a Day*, an adaptation of Beaumarchais' subtitle. In addition to adjusting the original text for English consumption with remarkable skill, Holcroft himself played the role of Figaro on the first night, in the absence of the actor Bonner who subsequently performed the part. Apparently both the play and its presentation caught public fancy, for, under date of December 28, the happy pirate wrote to his confederate Bonneville:

> I am sure you will pardon my apparent neglect when you remember how exceedingly hard I have been obliged to labour since my arrival in England. Figaro has made his appearance, and is likely to be as great a favourite in London as in Paris. I wish most sincerely you were here to be a witness of his good fortune. I enclose a letter of exchange for 480 livres on Girard and Co. bankers Paris.[13]

Holcroft could afford to be generous as he had received six hundred pounds for *The Follies of a Day*; and, having had the aplomb to copyright his version, he profited considerably from the publication of the play.

Although he adapted other French plays, Holcroft did not return to the Continent for ten years. Then in 1795, after his wild political

---

[12]W. P. Eaton, *The Actor's Heritage* (Boston, n.d.), pp. 42 ff., gives a vivid account of Holcroft's exploit.
[13]Hazlitt, *Complete Works*, III, p. 113.

statements had placed him in danger of imprisonment, he managed to escape to France in spite of the Revolution, thus gaining the distinction of being the only British actor to appear in France at that time. His volume of commentary, *Travels into France*, published in 1804, remains an interesting, though at times mordant, comment on the French, and particularly on what might be termed their national foibles.

6 · Beauty and the Beast

With the end of the Napoleonic wars in 1815 some influx of English players into France might have been anticipated, but a few private visits, notably by the Kembles, were all that took place. National emotions provide the most obvious explanation of this theatrical blank; we may assume that French feelings still ran much too high to permit successful visits by British companies although a few entertainers did appear individually during the next decade.

One of the first of these individuals from England figured both at home and across the Channel in a remarkable variety of activities. Lucia Bartolozzi was born in London in 1797 and at sixteen married Armand Vestris, a minor member of the great family of dancers. In spite of the fact that her fine contralto voice and personal beauty were of great promise for the stage, she had carried on her musical studies in a desultory fashion. Two brief seasons in London in Italian opera demonstrated her lack of background and inadequate training. None the less, Mme Vestris proceeded to a Paris début in December, 1816, at the Opéra Italien. The production, *Il Ratto de Prosperpine*, was the same in which she had made her first appearance in London.

The young artist's brief career in Paris is explained by a peculiar situation then existing at the Opéra Italien. The Italian prima donna, Catalini, after exhausting her popularity in England, had gone to France and with her husband, Valabrègue, had managed to obtain the privilege and subsidy of the Opéra Italien. Mme Catalini's intensely proud nature coupled with her impatience of any real rivalry quickly produced an unfortunate situation.

Coupling excessive pride and a complete lack of administrative experience, Mme Catalini chose to surround herself with mediocre figures convinced as she was that the prestige of her talent was sufficient to maintain the popularity of our Italian opera.[1]

The latter part of the comment concerns Valabrègue, whose cynical

---
[1] M. and L. Escudier, *Vie et aventures des cantatrices célèbres* (Paris, 1856), p. 22.

exploitation of his wife's voice is revealed by his remark: "My wife and four or five puppets are all we need." Valabrègue consequently recruited from England a group of performers who had either sunk into obscurity or never emerged from it. Thus a whole group of minor English singers appeared at the Théâtre Italien in 1816 and 1817: Mrs. Feron, who attempted to pose as Signora Feroni until her lack of Italian betrayed her; Mrs. Dickons, an actress and singer past her peak; and finally Mme Vestris herself. To do justice to Mme Catalini, it must be remarked that this spate of imports came while she was absent on tour.

Even against such modest competition Mme Vestris failed to distinguish herself at the Opéra Italien. She made her opening appearance with Mrs. Dickons, whom the critics damned with very faint praise. "Mme Dickons, who, it is reported, sings Italian without speaking it, without even understanding it, was formerly a great actress; today she is living on memories."[2] The younger débutante did not fare much better. In his summary of the deficiencies which he discerned at the Opéra, Sevelinges commented sharply:

It is not an Italian teacher but a music instructor that Mme Bartolozzi-Vestris would do well to consult if she really wants to belong to the new company. The stage has seen few prettier women than this young actress; so I am sure that her uncle the famous Bartolozzi would readily have put her in his engravings; but if he had been a theatre manager, would he have put her in his operas?[3]

Mme Vestris' appearances at the Opéra des Italiens were few in number and of slight importance. None the less, with the restless, intriguing nature that characterized her, she sought and obtained brief engagements at other theatres throughout the winter. Her biographer Grinsted is very gracious regarding these. "She had constant thought, however, of the profession to which she had been introduced," he writes, "and being a perfect mistress of the language frequently played at the French theatres both in tragedy and drama."[4] As the high point of these fleeting appearances she played opposite Talma in the role of Camille on a few occasions at the Théâtre Français. The great actor's Anglophil sympathies were at their liveliest at that time (in fact, his most noted English visit took place in the spring of

[2]K.Y.Z., *Almanach des spectacles pour Paris 1817* (Paris, 1818), under Italiens.
[3]C. D. Sevelinges, *Le Rideau levé* (Paris, 1818), p. 206.
[4]Cited in Charles Pearce, *Mme Vestris and Her Times* (London, 1923), p. 43.

1817). Consequently, we may perhaps safely attribute the young artist's ephemeral passage across the stage of the Comédie Française to personal indulgence on Talma's part.

Mme Vestris remained in Paris some two years longer, although her husband had long since sought refuge from his financial and marital disasters in bankruptcy and desertion. Early in 1820 she reappeared in London, where that indefatigable amateur of the theatre, William Pitt Lennox, credited himself with helping her to a début at Drury Lane.[5]

We discover another link between Mme Vestris and the French stage in the years immediately following her return to London. During the early twenties various groups of French actors presented plays to subscription audiences in Argyll Rooms, a Regent Street hall. Mme Vestris' command of French and her slight Continental experience made her useful in these presentations, and she took occasional parts in the actual performances.

Mme Vestris' relative failure in Paris originated in the weakness which she never really overcame, her lack of serious preparation. Her natural gifts sufficed to carry her only in the lightest of comic opera or in musical farce. George Vandenhoff, who went on the stage under her management, writes acidly, but justly, of her capacities:

She was accomplished though ignorant. She had begun her career with *éclat* as an Italian opera singer; she had afterwards played in Paris in French comedy; and she had latterly for many years been a standing favourite in the English theatres in characters requiring a certain *espiéglerie*, nearly allied to effrontery, together with fair musical capabilities—the *soubrette chantante* in fine.[6]

Obviously, an immature *soubrette chantante* did not suffice to satisfy the Paris public of 1817.

A minor but interesting phase of Anglo-French theatrical relations at this period appears in the amateur plays organized among the English occupation troops after Waterloo. The officers, of certain garrisons at least, whiled away their spare time by producing both light variety entertainments and more serious dramatic productions. A fair number of these amateur performers became professional actors after retiring from the army, and one at least, Frederick Yates, later returned to France in that capacity.

[5] W. P. Lennox, *Plays, Players and Playhouses* (London, 1881; 2 vols.), I, pp. 136–7.
[6] George Vandenhoff, *Leaves from an Actor's Notebook* (London, 1865), p. 4.

In the profuse memoirs of Lord William Pitt Lennox, whose mother organized the ball immortalized in *Childe Harold's Pilgrimage*, we learn that young Lennox himself was one of the amateurs. Even before Waterloo they had been busy organizing amateur presentations in Brussels. After the campaign of 1815, Lennox, then a lieutenant in the Duke of Wellington's personal staff, joined Frederick Yates, a junior officer from the Commissariat Department, in a strenuous attempt to organize private theatricals. The best quarters that they could find in Cambrai being a rickety loft above a horse stable, they had to fall back on what space they could obtain in Wellington's headquarters, the Château Cambrai. There, before the Iron Duke himself, Yates proved to be an excellent comedian and with other amateurs gave highly appreciated performances.[7] Although the two would-be actors did not obtain a suitable stage in 1816, it may be presumed that they eventually built one, for in the chronicles of the theatre at Cambrai we read of a temporary wooden structure on the Place aux Bois in which English actors presented plays in 1817.

Lennox and Yates maintained their dramatic enthusiasm by frequent visits to the officers' mess at Valenciennes. Here a large and eager amateur group had organized a first-class troupe which included several minor professional actresses brought from England to play the female roles. The leading actor, Cole, so developed his ability that he later turned professional under the name of Calcroft. Similarly, Prescott, playing under the name of Ward, developed into a polished and capable utility actor. Yates was a particularly welcome guest at Valenciennes not only because of his ability on the stage, but also because his remarkable powers as a mimic made him delightful after-dinner company. At one such gathering, however, he went beyond discretion and a rash imitation of Cole in that actor's favourite character came close to precipitating a duel.[8]

Yates was by no means unchallenged as a mimic. Among the Valenciennes officers, Benson Hill laid the foundation for his London career as a comedian by taking comedy parts in the occupation theatre. The plays were attended not only by the officers but also, on occasion, by the citizens of the town. At one of these public performances Hill who particularly enjoyed caricaturing Frenchmen, excelled himself

---

[7] W. P. Lennox, *Celebrities I Have Known* (London, 1867–7; 4 vols.), I, p. 255.
[8] *Ibid.*, p. 256.

to such a degree that the French members of his audience were thoroughly ruffled. One irate patriot demanded satisfaction at sword's point but fortunately was placated by the diplomacy of several of Hill's fellow officers.[9]

On the whole, these productions were fairly light but there were some more serious efforts. Cole's favourite role as young Norval in Home's popular drama, *Douglas*, roused much admiration and Benson Hill, the specialist in gay comedy, also made a strong impression on his audience as Bagatello in O'Keefe's *The Poor Soldier*. Nor was the troupe lacking in musical talent. Major Joseph Kelly, the brother of Michael Kelly, who had acted in and composed incidental music for many plays, went from Cambrai to strengthen the Valenciennes players; he and Fairfield of that garrison took the chief roles in a presentation of *The Beggar's Opera*, Kelly as Captain Macheath, Fairfield as Peachum, the confederate of the thieves. In addition, in the interval between the play and a following farce, the two often entertained the audience with popular duet numbers.

Only one of these officers who later became professional actors, requires further attention. Frederick Yates, already mentioned, returned to England in 1817 and, on the advice of Charles Mathews, resolved to enter the acting profession. Charles Mathews (or the Elder Mathews as he is sometimes called, to distinguish him from his actor son Charles James Mathews) ranked with Liston as the leading English comedian of the early nineteenth century. In addition to the usual talents of the comic player, he possessed an amazing power of mimicry and pantomime; indeed a number of his favourite roles required him to portray several different personages in one play, and he also sang, recited, and at times ventriloquized: he was in fact almost a whole troupe in himself. He frequently made provincial tours with a small supporting cast, sometimes with only his wife. His variety entertainments or "At Homes," as he called them, achieved considerable success as a type of intimate revue. Mathews had met his younger partner at a costume ball where Yates, who had come in the costume of a role in which Mathews often distinguished himself, proceeded to entertain the company with a series of imitations of actors, ending with Mathews himself. Struck by Yates' talent, Mathews urged the young man to join him on the stage. Since Yates, both in his amateur performances and

[9]Lennox, *Plays, Players and Playhouses*, II, p. 115.

in his later career, had the reputation of an inimitable mimic, it is evident that these two who set out for France in 1817 constituted a pantomime company in themselves. Yates had already spent some time in France and had learned a certain amount of reasonably correct French, and Mathews as a boy had attended a French school in London in which he had acquired considerable facility in the spoken language. The brief excursion of 1817 was probably planned by Yates, for it consisted largely of a return visit to his former army haunts.

The two actors crossed to Calais and in the English theatre at Boulogne gave a single performance of George Colman's *Sylvester Doggerwood* to a disappointingly small house. They then moved on by post-chaise to Cambrai, Mathews gathering material for his sketch, *A Trip to Paris*, as he admired with amusement the braggadocio antics of the postillions.[10] At Cambrai they received a warm welcome from Lord Hill, the commandant of the city and gave two performances in the temporary hall already referred to. The day after Christmas, Mathews was delighted at being invited to dinner by Wellington at the Château Saint Martin and he and Yates gave two performances for the duke's staff and guests in the theatrical hall arranged at the château. A private letter of the time written from Cambrai gives some interesting comment on the players and their reception:

Great festivities have been going forward this Christmas at the headquarters of the British Army. The Duke of Wellington has had his château (twelve miles from here) crowded with visitors. The officers of the staff have performed several dramatic pieces with great effect. Mathews has been out here and was invited by the Duke to the Château; he gave (here) his celebrated "Mail Coach Adventures" and also his "Actor of All Work." The temporary theatre is very neatly fitted up.[11]

The two-man troupe arrived at Valenciennes on the last day of the year, and, on the first two days of January, performed at the theatre in which the British officer actors were alternating with a French company. Then, since the French players had engaged the hall for the following two days and both men were due to appear in Scotland early in January, they returned at once to England apparently much pleased with their visit.

For some time Mathews had been dissatisfied with the roles allotted to him at the Lyceum Theatre, feeling that he was being dismissed

---

[10]Mrs. Anne Mathews, *Memoirs of Charles Mathews, Comedian* (London, 1839; 4 vols.), IV, pp. 32 ff.

[11]Cited by Mrs. Anne Mathews, *ibid.*, p. 34.

as a mere mimic rather than regarded as a serious actor. Consequently, he decided to attempt independent presentations of his programmes, and placed himself under the management of a Mr. Arnold. Early in May, 1819, with his new associate, Mathews paid a brief visit to Paris which filled him with admiration. At the Théâtre des Variétés, he saw "three of the finest actors I have ever beheld, Tiercelin, Brunet and Potier." Finally, to crown his visit, he was the dinner guest of the universally admired Talma. The tangible result of this journey was the celebrated sketch, *A Journey to Paris*, in which his droll comments kept audiences laughing heartily for years.

Some seven years later in February, 1827, while in Paris on a business trip, Yates made two appearances in the concert hall of M. Comte, who maintained a regular attraction under the title of *Le Spectacle de M. Comte*. Our chief source of information on the matter, the incorrigibly Anglophobe journal *Le Courrier des théâtres*, curtly announced that an English pantomimist, Mr. Yates, being in Paris, was acceding to requests in giving that evening, February 9, a performance entitled *Les Réminiscences de Yates*. It compared him with French performers of the same category, and also asserted that he was held superior to Mathews in the field of variety entertainment. The *Courrier* concluded by stating that one performance only was scheduled. Reporting briefly on the event, the journal denied Yates any originality, accused him of monotony, and suggested that the applause came from his English hearers.

A repeat appearance was decided on, and the *Courrier* of February 11 duly rallied Mr. Yates on his "unique" concert, giving him a second thrust on the succeeding day when its ire had been aroused by his proposed imitation of Talma in the role of Oreste. Happily the visitor cancelled this proposal, in view of the recent death of the great tragedian. His programme, as advertised on the 14th, included the usual stage coach adventures, scenes at the fair, pawn shop episodes, and an imaginary dialogue between the actors Kean and Young. In its final report, still chaffing Yates on his "unique" performance, the relentless *Courrier* again suggested that his appeal was wholly for the English and concluded: "Mr. Yates should be pleased at having visited Paris. His English customers paid for his trip. Now let him begone."

Yates did go to England since he had to return to his duties as manager of the Adelphi Theatre, but in 1829 he returned to Paris accompanied by Mathews. Again the two made a relatively brief stay in France.

Announcing the arrival of Mathews and his companion, the *Courrier* extended its cordiality to the unexpected length of giving the lie to its own comments of 1827 and referring to Yates' former appearances as having been followed "with equal keenness by his fellow countrymen and by the inhabitants of the capital." The visitors opened at the Théâtre Italien on September 10 under the auspices of Emile Laurent, a staunch Anglophil manager. The modest theatre was ideally suited for the intimate type of entertainment in which Mathews felt most at ease. Both performers proved highly popular, especially with their numerous compatriots in the audience.

The critic of the *Globe* apparently found them fascinating and described the evening as "an interesting and worthwhile entertainment." Accurately characterizing them as highly original satirical mime artists, he compared them with the French comedians, Perlet and Joly. He admitted to being somewhat baffled by Mathews' major efforts, not only because his command of English was insufficient for him to cope with the many changes of accent, but also because in many cases the types parodied, being English, were not familiar to him. Mathews' favourite number, *A Journey in a Stage Coach*, introduced a considerable number of such parodies. A little comedy played by the two actors and a set of mannequins, with Yates doing valiant work, gave the critics more amusement. The high point of the evening for the French patrons was the series of imitations given by Yates in which Terry, Kean, Macready, and other English actors familiar to many of the audience from the 1827–8 visits were mimicked with startling and amusing fidelity.

Their performance on the 12th featured *The Youthful Days of Mr. Mathews* and *Stop Thief*, a little play in which Yates took all the various roles. The comment of *Figaro* discriminated between this and other comic gifts:

Mr. Mathews is a superior man, who must not be confused with vulgar comics who, under the name of mimics, give a crude caricature of our customs and our leading personalities. He has good taste, wit, sparkle, and originality. He seems to gain his effects effortlessly; he is a delicate comedian such as Potier would be if he were English.

The reviewer continued with a good personal description, then gave a brief *résumé* of the autobiographical sketch given by Mathews and commented: "His face, indeed his whole person, are like wax, moulded at will by his thoughts."

The great critic Philarète Chasles, recalling performances of Mathews which he had witnessed, also commented pertinently on his particular gifts. "He was not a comic author or actor, not a caricaturist; but a complex and highly curious example of English civilization and of the minute analysis of which that country has given us so many models." The charge of trifling superficiality sometimes directed at Mathews, he refuted directly, describing Mathews as being "gifted with the keenest and most penetrating comic perception and with the rarest gifts of mimicry; nor does his penetration halt at the surface; his was a creative instinct, his observation was personal." Chasles suggested further that the France of 1839 "is approaching the same type of cold observation and ironically detailed imitation which characterized Charles Mathews.[12] It would be hazardous to suggest that Mathews' brief appearance had anything to do with this development, but Chasles' contention is interesting to remember in viewing the critical comedies of the Second Empire in which we find exactly this mixture of close observation and comic-ironic comment.

Another member of His Majesty's forces to go on the stage and later appear in Paris belonged to the navy. This actor, Thomas Cooke by name, was released from the service in 1802. After an insignificant début at the Royal Theatre he went to Astley's Amphitheatre, playing (rather appropriately) Lord Nelson in one of their spectacular productions. During the next two decades Cooke developed the capacity and the reputation for playing the weird or monster roles in such melodramas as *The Castle Spectre*, *The Vampire*, and *Presumption, or The Fate of Frankenstein*. This dramatization of Mrs. Shelley's famous novel appeared at the Lyceum in 1823.

Cooke's special success in *The Fate of Frankenstein*, coupled with the vogue for melodramatic mystery plays in Paris, encouraged Merle, the ambitious manager of the Porte-Saint-Martin theatre, to engage him for the summer season of 1826. After several mimed roles during April and May, Cooke launched a triumphal run as the monster in *Le Monstre et le Magicien*, the French adaptation of *Frankenstein*. Merle and his associates had transformed Mrs. Shelley's tragedy into a three-act *mélodrame féerie à grand spectacle* complete with a ballet and concluding with an impressive catastrophe in the form of a tempest.[13]

[12]Philarète Chasles, *Revue de Paris* (March, 1839).
[13]*Le Monstre et le Magicien, mélodrame féerie en trois actes à grand spectacle, par MM. Merle et Antony: Musique de M. Alevarni* (Paris, 1826).

The play scored an undisputed success at its opening performance on June 10, the Parisians finding Cooke's monster quite as blood-curdling as London audiences had three years previously. Described in Merle's version as a *personnage muet*, the monster, after a thunderous irruption onto the scene at the close of the first act, marked his subsequent half-dozen appearances by elaborately pantomimed admiration, grief, pain, and rage, and threw the more susceptible members of the audience into convulsions of fear and horror. So great was the enthusiasm for the early performances that from the fourth of July *Le Monstre* was presented continuously as the evening bill through the hot weather season.

Cooke was not, however, bound to one role. On July 15, in a vaudeville revue given at the theatre, he contributed a scene in English from *The Pilot*, a play in which he had performed the winter before. On September 2 a special benefit performance was given for the visiting artist, the programme including *Le Monstre*, a vaudeville, and a ballet pantomime, *Le Déserteur*, in which Cooke took the title role. The receipts of the performance totalled thirty-six hundred francs, a gratifying sum compared with the usual proceeds from such events. This very successful engagement, which had reached eighty performances, ended with a final presentation of *Le Monstre* on the tenth of September. The artist then returned to London for the winter season. The *Courrier des théâtres* had done its best to speed Cooke's departure by announcing it prematurely several times, but had succeeded only in doing the theatre the best turn possible by sarcastically urging all those who wished to see *Le Monstre* to rush to the wicket. "The twenty-eighth of this month Mr. Cooke will return to London. So you must hurry to see, or to see again, the famous monster whom the ticket seller considers as handsome as Cupid. Such are the powers of filthy lucre."[14] The last performance, a supplementary appearance, was by public demand and it is interesting to find that the melodrama in which the Englishman had won such a triumph soon appeared on the bills again at the Porte-Saint-Martin. Less than eight weeks later the French actor Gobert assumed the role created by his British predecessor and enjoyed a long run in it.

Much of Cooke's Parisian triumph was owing to the early Romantic fascination for the weird and the horrific which was then sweeping

[14] *Le Courrier des théâtres*, Paris, August 24, 1826.

the capital. Vampires, haunted castles, ghosts, and skeletons, all the natural and supernatural horrors of the English Gothic novels and their French equivalents, the *romans noirs*, crowded the boards of the secondary theatres. Shakespeare himself did not escape; it became very easy to dismiss him from serious literary consideration by underlining the superficial resemblances between his historical tragedies and the melodramatic ferocities of the Théâtre Ambigu and the Porte-Saint-Martin.

A further indication of the popularity of *Le Monstre et le Magicien* was given by the parodies which promptly appeared in other boulevard theatres. *Le Spectacle de M. Comte* presented a group of junior actors in *Le Monstre et le Physicien* which continued for some time after Cooke's departure. The Théâtre de la Gaîté followed shortly with *Le Petit Monstre*, which held its place on the bills until the end of November.[15] Strictly speaking, this play was not a parody since it had been given two years earlier although its revival was obviously an attempt to catch popular attention by the title.

[15] *Ibid., passim* August-November, 1826.

7 · "Once More Unto the Breach..."

The last day of July, 1822, witnessed the first presentation of English plays in France by a full company of British actors. The attempt took place under the direction of a courageous pioneer, Mr. S. Penley. Unfortunately, any artistic reactions which the occasion might have aroused were obliterated by an outburst of jingoistic spleen on the part of the public. Hence, we can scarcely consider the evening as a literary event; we might in fact regard it almost as a petty international incident.

Initially, Mr. Penley had requested M. Merle, the Anglophil director of the Porte-Saint-Martin theatre, for a one-week engagement in which to present English plays. Merle welcomed his proposed guest, but reminded him of the administrative requirements. Hence, Penley addressed a humble petition to the English ambassador in Paris, seeking his aid in gaining official sanction for the project. Permission arrived in due course, with the condition that all plays which Penley proposed to present must be submitted in advance to the censors.

Up to this point all seemed to be going well, and accordingly the opening performance was announced. Yet Mr. Penley's enthusiasm now considerably exceeded his tact, as the wording of his bills reveals: "By His Britannic Majesty's most humble servants will be performed the tragedy of *Othello* in five acts by the most celebrated Shakespeare." The ill-advised nature of such phrasing seems obvious. To flaunt His Britannic Majesty before liberals to whom monarchy, at home or abroad, was at the moment equally detestable, invited opposition; to flaunt him in the faces of the chauvinists who, in 1822, because of Napoleon's recent death, vehemently detested anything British, invited disaster. In literary circles the term "the most celebrated Shakespeare" looked very like a gratuitous slight on the nation to whom Corneille, Racine, and Molière represented the pinnacle of dramatic art.

Public interest was, however, running high as *Le Réveil* reported: "From four o'clock on, an immense throng was clamouring at the doors of the theatre, all the loges were reserved." *L'Album* commented briefly: "The English actors will open tomorrow at the Porte-Saint-Martin theatre in *Othello*. The *dilettanti* will doubtless rush to attend the play; it is only in French that *Othello* offends them."

Merle certainly could not complain with regard to the financial aspects of his opening night. The house was crammed and the great crowds about the theatre demanding entrance were kept in order only by an exceptional array of *gendarmes*. But the financial return was the only satisfactory aspect of the evening; the *parterre* in particular, and also many other occupants of the theatre, had come with the intention of killing the play. Jeers, raucous guffaws, animal cries, and booing largely drowned out the first attempts on the part of the players. However, when the actor Pierson came on the stage to ask if the public wished to hear the play, a large number did call for a hearing. Consequently, amid much dissension in the audience, the actors managed to wrestle their way to the end of the first act to the irritation of the more rabid factions. *Le Réveil*, obviously a fairly impartial journal, maintained that "the sensible majority of the public defended the players and wanted to get their money's worth" and described the brawling disturbers as "a mob of tu'penny judges." It recognized the purpose of the uproar but held that a more dignified protest would have been defensible. "An empty hall would have shown more national spirit than the disgraceful scenes of last night."

To add to the general turbulence, during the intermission the discovery of the notorious polemist Martainville in one of the loges created a near riot. Lukewarm in his allegiance to Napoleon, and accused of collaboration with the allies after Waterloo, Martainville was precisely the man to fan the flames of animosity. Controversy being his very life, he proceeded in round terms and with insulting epithets to harangue the agitators on their misbehaviour. Police intervention finally imposed sufficient order for an attempt at the second act. Here Barton as Othello managed to wring a burst of applause from the less fanatic members of the audience. This tribute, however, precipitated a general *mêlée* of fisticuffs, fainting ladies, and police cordons. Even the appearance of the English actresses on the stage produced no distraction; the mob determinedly howled them down. When the courageous company then stood their ground in silence on the stage, the traditional eggs and vegetables, accompanied by a weird assortment of copper coins, pipe-stems, and other objects, began to fly.

The performers tried to save something of the evening for those who did wish to hear Shakespeare by omitting a large portion of the play and jumping to the last act. Worse disaster awaited them there. *Le Miroir* voiced French opinion quite accurately. "It is the shocking catastrophe of that splendid but strange tragedy which makes up the last act. We witnessed it in all its horror. The grotesqueness of this revolting scene, a scene such as rarely appears on the stage, was enough to grate on the sensibilities of the spectators, and it did." The smothering of Desdemona, a scene calculated to offend even the most ardent French admirer of Shakespeare by its defiance of the classic proprieties, precipitated a final barrage from the *parterre* which brought down the curtain.

In the French tradition, the troupe had intended to close the bill with a comedy, *The Rendez-vous*, an English adaptation of a play by Feydeau. But on their reappearance the exasperated chauvinists drove them from the stage, Miss Gaskill fainting from having received a copper sou full in the face. *Le Miroir* sharply condemned what little of the play was presented: "The way in which the actors played it transformed it into a display barely worthy of the fairs." Miss Penley was described as lacking nobility of bearing, while her younger sister, who displayed more energy and expression, lacked elegance. Amusingly enough, all the men, though given short shrift artistically, were unintentionally knighted, being referred to as "Sir."

The critic for *L'Album*, after lamenting the popular excesses, managed to formulate some comments on the performance as such: "Mr. Penley's performance seemed vigorous and convincing. Mr. Barton, who carried the role of Othello, lacks nobility, but there was some warmth in his delivery. The younger Miss Penley as Emilia shows sensitivity." Speaking in a more general fashion of the play, the critic concluded with some justice: "In general, English tragedy and its interpretation are so foreign to our tastes and customs that we can scarcely be impartial judges in this matter." He condemned the handling of the comedy quite as severely as did *Le Miroir*: "As for the comedy, we dare to state that our lowest comedians would handle it as well as the actors of His Britannic Majesty."

Two days later the company again tried their fortunes. To avoid any difficulties over Shakespeare, they chose Sheridan's *The School for Scandal*, and a second item, *The Road to Bath*; in the hope of excluding the rougher elements, prices were doubled. Neither precaution availed; there were not seats enough for all those who demanded places, and the assault began on the opening lines of the play with disastrous effect. This time it was not Shakespeare who bore the brunt of the jeers but the English in general and the hardy actors in particular. As host to the intruders, Merle found himself obliged to appear on the stage to apologize for his share in the matter. The mob then noisily awaited two French plays to replace the offending English bill. During the intermission the seekers after trouble promptly found it. After having spent the bulk of the intermission in ejecting the persistent Martainville from the theatre and in smashing the instruments of the orchestra, the more hot-blooded among them demanded an appearance from Merle, and not being satisfied, launched an attack on the stage itself. Here a company of armed police awaited them; in the pitched battle which ensued casualties to both the combatants and the furniture reached considerable proportions. Meanwhile a rioting crowd outside the theatre building was being cleared away by cavalry charges.

The affair had obviously lost any potential literary significance and was developing into a test of strength between the authorities and an obstreperous element. Naturally, the police officials did not wish to show any signs of capitulation by ordering the performances to be cancelled. Higher counsel, however, did not concur with this firm attitude, and the Merle-Penley experiment concluded at that point, wrecked on the rock of nationalistic prejudice. The journals of the day, with little real literary material on which to exercise their powers debated rather the nature and justification of the reception. The radical nationalists hailed the rioters as patriotic heroes and suggested that they represented public resentment of foreign intruders. A larger number of those most actively engaged in obstruction were in fact former army men and, probably feeling that they were continuing the battles of the *grande armée*, shouted for Shakespeare's dismissal as a lieutenant of Wellington. There were, however, moderate commentators who deplored the behaviour of the radicals, or who hopefully affirmed that the *parterre* did not really represent general opinion.

Neither France nor England had any record for hospitality in welcoming each other's performers. From the days of Charles the First, when the Queen's French dancers occasioned much scandal, through the similar protests under Charles the Second and the brawls of 1749 against Parisian troupes in London, to the disgraceful skirmishing of soldiers and civilians in the very presence of George III in 1763, the English public had displayed their antipathy to French artists. Nevertheless, had the disturbers of the peace in 1822 been impartial, they would have had to admit that a considerable number of French players had recently made both popular and profitable appearances in London.

The violence of the political animus overshadowed a second factor in the situation, which did exert some influence. The battle developing between the Classicists and the Romantics would have made the presentation of Shakespeare on the Paris stage a test case had the two parties been able to clash on a literary basis around a series of performances at the Porte-Saint-Martin. Thus, although it was the chauvinists whose violence dominated the situation, we may be certain that the more literary groups, though less uproarious, were by no means unanimously cordial. All in all, it was painfully apparent that in August, 1822, the Paris public was far from ready to consider Shakespeare or any English dramatist or English player on his own merits. "Sir Penley's company or any other," wrote the *Miroir* correspondent, "must give up any idea of gaining a hearing in a public theatre in France."

The directors of the Porte-Saint-Martin publicly withdrew from the affair in a letter addressed to *Le Réveil* on August 4.

In making arrangements with the director of the English company for six performances of British dramatic masterpieces we thought that we would please the public; we were mistaken. Our one aim, our first responsibility being to please it, we had to halt the performances as soon as public opinion showed itself overwhelmingly. The ensuing events were out of our control.

Respectfully,

DESSERRE and MERLE, Joint Directors.

In the face of the inevitable, Mr. Penley made a limited withdrawal. On August 10, in the *Journal de Galignani*, he addressed an open letter to the public, announcing his hope of continuing performances and also of bringing the great Edmund Kean to Paris as a guest performer. The first advertisements outlined a group of six performances to be presented on a subscription basis in a small privately owned hall in the Rue Chantereine. Here, with more control over the attendance, it was possible to eliminate hostile interference and the proposed run of two weeks, beginning on August 20, extended into a season of over two months.

The genuine admirers of English drama attended a representative series of plays. *Romeo and Juliet, Hamlet, Othello,* and *Richard III* were the Shakespearean tragedies presented. The non-Shakespeare tragedies included: *The Castle Spectre* adapted from "Monk" Lewis's novel; *Guy Mannering*, another Romantic adaptation, from Scott; and Rowe's *Jane Shore*, then enjoying much popularity in England. Among the dramas we find *Wallace*, the standard play *Douglas*, and Kotzebue's international favourite *The Stranger*. Since a double bill was usually presented the company also gave a considerable range of comedies: *The Taming of the Shrew, The Honeymoon,* farces such as *The Wedding Day, Three Weeks after Marriage, The Mayor of Garret,* and half a dozen others. Determined to use every possible appeal, the players even experimented with incidental songs and one or two attempts at operettas. A declamation of Dryden's *Alexander's Feast*, by Bromley in Greek costume, was warmly received. The classical character of both poem and presentation probably explains this cordiality.

The genuine *amateurs* both English and French, though not numerous, were very faithful in their attendance and warmly appreciative. The *Réveil* for August 22 reported: "The little hall where the English players have taken refuge was practically filled." Hopes that attendance would increase were encouraged by the remark of the same journal on the thirtieth of that month to the effect that: "It might be that in time the English plays might develop a kind of vogue." Though attendance varied sharply, the enthusiasts for English drama supported the troupe in Paris until late October and even then their departure was not because of desertion by the public. Hoping to remain in the the capital throughout the winter, Penley petitioned the authorities to extend his season and asked for permission to give two plays a week in a larger hall, the Salle Louvois. His request was refused. In consequence, the last presentation, which was described as Mr. Penley's benefit performance, took place on October 25. In two months at the Rue Chantereine the company had given over two dozen different plays ranging from tragedy to farce; had somewhat rashly attempted two short comic operas; had taken *Jane Shore* to the theatre at Versailles; and they had paid their way.

English drama had, however, been introduced under conditions that were far from ideal. The Chantereine hall was small, primarily intended only for private concerts, and with only meagre stage facilities. Chided by the critics for not offering more Shakespeare, Penley unwillingly presented *Romeo and Juliet*, an experiment which convinced everyone of the impossibility of doing justice to the great English dramatist on the tiny Rue Chantereine stage. Moreover, in spite of earlier claims respecting the calibre of his company, Mr. Penley did not head a distinguished cast. Although not much more than a good utility actor, he frequently took the chief parts himself, supported by his daughters in the feminine roles. The entire group totalled some seventeen or eighteen persons, none of whom ever gained much reputation on the stage. In short, the plays were presented by a mediocre company striving under unfavourable stage conditions to offer a taxing array of dramas. None the less, one must admire their courage in the face of public and official obstruction.

The obstacles were not merely in securing a hall. Mr. Penley, in company with the Paris managers, had also to bear with the phenomenon of Restoration censorship. The stern laws against the freedom of the press had their counterparts in the severity of control over the stage, since, in order to utilize the theatres for its own purposes, the government not only curbed their freedom but also strove to use them as vehicles for propaganda. The censors maintained a zealous watch over the dignity of the throne, the nobility, the government, and, in general, of people in office or with well-lined pockets. Political discussion was frowned upon; morals were required to be painfully high; the violence of the melodramas which abounded in 1822 was deplored and checked as far as possible. By an unhappy coincidence, Penley encountered the censorship precisely when a change towards increased rigour was being made. The chief additional restriction of 1822 affected the type of report demanded from those reading the plays, the new regulation requiring a detailed outline and verdict on each play.

Ironically, it was an unusually innocuous offering which came to grief. Penley had submitted an innocent comedy, *John Bull*, by George Colman, who had been British censor of plays for some time. The French censors expressed themselves as being scandalized at the profligacy and knavery attributed to the rich and great in the play, and saw no reason why virtue, honesty, and independence should be represented as belonging to the poor. The Prefect of Police instructed Penley to cancel his proposed presentation of *John Bull* and to substitute a less indecent play. Even in 1822, however, *Le Miroir* deprecated the ban and on September 4, its critic wrote of the play: "It is the most romantic, comical, and moral of plays." He suggested that it should be given; and an edition was actually printed for sale.

Artistically, the results of the Chantereine season were more or less mediocre. A faithful group of earnest Anglophils and *amateurs* of English drama, text in hand, had followed with mingled pleasure and amazement the new and strange dramas, which some of them felt must furnish the models for a rejuvenated French theatre. The Comédiens Français also honoured the visitors by their presence and applause. Mlle Mars and Talma, the pillars of the Comédie Française, stood completely above nationalistic bickering, Talma especially being well known for his English sympathies.

Although the critics were free to become acquainted with live English drama, the press took no great notice of it except to express mild satisfaction at the exclusion of the violently obstructionist elements and to adopt a generally benevolent attitude. To be fair, the Parisian critics of 1822, even those sympathetically inclined, were hardly capable of appreciating the English drama either by their knowledge of it or by their command of English. They tended, in consequence, to confine themselves to general remarks on such matters as the intrigues of the plays. These they usually considered barbarous, grotesque, wearying, even preposterous, although occasionally they admitted their power. Feeling more competent to judge the actors, they regularly did so but their judgments bore more frequently on the bearing and pantomime of the players than on the interpretation of the roles. The Misses Penley usually fared best in the criticism. On August 26, *Le Miroir* commented:

Miss Penley, who until the present had shown herself simply as a graceful and intelligent actress, proved the evening before last, while playing the role of the guilty Jane

Shore, that she does possess genuine sensitivity, remarkable vigour, a naturalness which avoids vulgarity, nobility without affectation; she impressed us as a gifted tragedian. Her touching pantomime ... wrung tears from the whole audience.

In a burst of admittedly justified self-righteousness he added:

Frequent applause made it plain to Miss Penley that in France talent always finds unbiased appreciation and enthusiastic admirers.

The impact on Paris cannot, however, be considered as having been appreciable, judging from the reactions of the various *Almanachs des spectacles*, the semi-official compendium of dramatic activity in Paris for the year. One, compiled by Antoine Coupart, did not consider the Porte-Saint-Martin *débâcle* worth mention. In the introduction to the section on the popular theatres, however, the author directed an oblique thrust which may have been intended for any admirers of the English players: "Romantic balderdash is striving to intrude on our noble tragic stage; at the same time one may see in our popular theatres the melodramatic effusions of Walter Scott."[1] Less agitated by the literary situation, the *Almanach des spectacles de K.Y.Z.* takes a mildly jocular attitude. Summing up the year for the Porte-Saint-Martin as reasonably successful, it lists among M. Merle's reverses "especially his ludicrous English actors." For a wide variety of reasons, neither critics nor public were ready to appreciate Shakespeare, English drama, or English artists.

The dogged determination of the *parterre* not to listen to English voices did not, however, discourage one group (the young avant-garde dramatists of Paris), a group which for some time had been assiduously encouraging the appearance of British drama before the public. "One of the plays given by the English company in the little Rue Chantereine theatre," wrote the *Miroir* critic on September 14, "has inspired a dozen authors who are busy having it translated in order to have it given at the theatres of the Boulevard." It is pleasant to discover at least one literary influence, slight and wraithlike though it may be.

Penley's experiences did not completely discourage English managers, for within a year, in October 1823, Joseph Smithson of the Theatre Royal petitioned Sir Charles Stuart, English ambassador at

[1] Coupart Antoine, *Almanach des spectacles depuis le commencement du 19ᵉ siècle, pour l'an 1823* (Paris, 1823), p. 192.

Paris, to give his official support to a request for a licence "for the performance of a select Company of English Comedians in France under my management." Smithson gave his assurance as to the talent and personal character of his players along with suitable references. Sir Charles, whose enthusiasm was probably restrained by his recollection of the fate suffered by the last players whom he had sponsored, did his official duty by passing on the letter to the Director of Police. The hazy recollection of the facts in the Penley case held by the official entrusted with deciding on Smithson's merits appears in the latter portion of his report to the Director of Police. He opposed the opening of any new theatre on the grounds that there were, in his opinion, quite enough places of entertainment in Paris and continued:

> But if Mr. Smithson wished to renew the attempt made a few years ago by an English actor, he probably might obtain permission from the Minister to give plays by subscription in a theatre already in operation provided he had made arrangements with the director of that theatre as Mr. Thierney had made with the director of the Porte-Saint-Martin.[2]

In this functionary's mind a scant fourteen months had become some years; the open sale of tickets, many of which had been purchased by antagonistic rioters when Penley's troupe had appeared at the Porte-Saint-Martin, had become a subscription series. The magisterial mishandling of the unfortunate Penley's very name furnishes a good example of the French tendency to take liberties with English nomenclature. The reply to the ambassador curtly regretted that the number of theatres already in operation prevented the authorities from granting the request.

A brief lull in the battle for an appearance by English companies on the Paris stage was terminated by the man who had opened the campaign. The visit of Thomas Cooke in 1826 made a deep impression upon the managers of the Porte-Saint-Martin and in particular upon Merle. This inveterate supporter of the English determined to have the London actors make a second visit in the following year. Unfortunately, Merle lost the direction of the theatre at that point. His successor, Emile Laurent, shared his enthusiasm, however, and in December, 1826, he managed to secure official consent for establishing in Paris a permanent English theatrical company on the firm basis of

[2]*La Revue germanique*, issue of May-June 1908, "Smithson et un théâtre anglais à Paris," contains a full account of this incident.

subscription support. Two problems remained: to obtain an English troupe, and to locate an available hall.

The first was solved with little difficulty. Frederick Yates, whom we have met as the actor, and then manager of the Adelphi Theatre, readily agreed to bring a company and early in 1827 came to Paris to aid in obtaining accommodation for them. Laurent officially requested the director of the department of Beaux-Arts that they might share the theatre hall of the Opéra Italien, and Yates made a special personal appeal to the Dauphiness to use her good offices on their behalf, but neither was successful and permission was denied. Yates retired from the scene at this point. But Laurent persisted, and, discouraging as his struggles had been, his moment of triumph was approaching.

8 · Shakespeare, Smithson, Shore, and Company

Among the chief factors favourable to the visit of the English players in 1827 was the condition of French drama in the eighteen-twenties. To all but the fanatical (a considerable group it must be admitted) it was apparent that the classical theatre had sunk to a moribund state. The glories of the classical school had swiftly declined in the eighteenth century, and the most ardent admirer of the great masters, Voltaire himself, produced only wooden imitations of Racine. The natural evolution of a new form, however, was disturbed in the convulsions of the Revolution and Empire. There were, in 1795, some members of the public who viewed themselves as modern Romans and for them the classical plays seemed to have a certain actuality. The political subjects treated by Corneille and Voltaire were imitated by authors who felt obliged to play a part in France's effort to maintain her place in Europe; hence, political discussions such as those of Corneille held some meaning for authors and public.

But, although a fair number of plays on the classical model were produced during the Empire, vitality was really to be found in the new and popular melodrama. The works of Pixérécourt and Caigniez illustrate that in the early years of the nineteenth century the French public, while history was being made in such violent fashion, demanded strong theatrical fare. Yet the citadels of classicism, and especially those of criticism, stood firm; to the critics the tenets of Boileau and Voltaire remained unalterable. In 1810, for the edification of his son and other earnest young men, Pierre Adolphe Capelle published his ample *Dictionnaire de Morale, de Science et de littérature, ou Choix de pensées ingénieuses et sublimes, de dissertations et de définitions; Extraites des plus célèbres moralistes, orateurs, poètes et savants.* Among the "pensées ingénieuses et sublimes" we find the following effort by the compiler himself: "England has produced a limited number of tragic authors, among whom we distinguish Shakespeare, who displays sparks of genius but of a crude uncultivated order; and Addison, who is more correct and more submissive to the rules of drama."[1]

The continued reflection of Voltaire's verdict on Shakespeare as a barbarous genius is apparent here; Addison's estimable but lifeless classical tragedy *Cato* would, of course, win the approval of such a traditionalist. But M. Capelle's opinion, misguided as it seems, is significant, not only because of its relationship to Voltaire's, but also because it represented a considerable body of critical belief.

A more plausible but no less firm opinion is set forth in *La Minerve française* of May 1818. The writer, modestly cloaking himself as M. XXX, contends that the theatre of a country is one of its most distinctive national productions and should be cherished as such. According to him, nationality has to be the basis on which any theatre is built.

Before proving to Frenchmen that they are wrong in admiring Corneille and Racine; to Englishmen that they should not idolize Shakespeare; to Germans that Schiller and Goethe are far from being universally admirable; or Spaniards that Calderon and Lope de Vega, though sometimes brilliant, are ill disciplined, you would have to begin by demonstrating to them that they should cease being French, English, German, or Spanish.

He deprecates dramatic importation feeling that each nation should cultivate its theatrical garden in peace, since, he maintains: "To attempt to contradict a nation's conceptions regarding its own theatre is to undertake the most fruitless task possible." With equal enthusiasm he justifies the physically static debate which constitutes French classical drama. A nation in which the art of brilliant analytic conversation has reached the excellence attained in France will, he declares, inevitably demand a conversational type of play. The English, who have not attained such a high level of cultural development, demand dramas of pictorial action which reflect their physically active society. He concludes triumphantly: "If anything clearly proves that the Revolution while improving French customs has not changed them, it is the fact that their worship of Molière, Corneille, Racine, and Voltaire remains the same, or more accurately that it has increased."

The Capelles and the contributors to *La Minerve française* did not, however, monopolize the scene; the cosmopolitan outlook, marked before the Revolution, grew steadily among the younger groups.

[1] W. P. Lennox, *Plays, Players and Playhouses* (London, 1881; 2 vols.), II, pp. 176–7.

The Revolution ended theatrical monopoly in Paris, and one result was an enormous increase in the number of theatres accompanied by a good deal of moderately radical experimentation. In 1806, for example, the actors in one of the new theatres—the Théâtre Molière, founded in 1791—in order to capitalize on the vogue for foreign plays, decided to devote themselves exclusively to presenting these works in translation. They hoped thus not only to recoup their own fortunes but also to help revivify French literature. The name of the theatre was changed to the Théâtre des Variétés Etrangères and its company opened in November to a large audience.

They announced to the audience that Sheridan, Garrick, Schiller, Calderon, Goldoni would in turn enrich our stage; that Aristotle's unities would often be violated, that we would journey from one country to another as in the Arabian Nights and that during the intermission characters would age by fifty years if such was their fancy.[2]

The faintly sarcastic tone of this review was reflected in public support; the new venture lasted only eight months. Yet in that period the actors managed to stage over sixty plays, most by the German author, Kotzebue. The translations were apparently somewhat cavalier, to judge from the critics' passionate protests against the massacre of the dramas concerned.

English dramatists, especially Shakespeare, had also suffered cruelly from their translators in the eighteenth century. Judicious Frenchmen from Voltaire to Gide have stressed the difficulties of translating Shakespeare, and certainly thorny problems do face his translators. In the versions of his plays produced by Letourneur in 1766, and especially in the classical arrangements which Ducis made from them, English lovers of Shakespeare would hardly have recognized his work at all. With other foreign masters the great dramatist received somewhat better handling in the eighteen-twenties. At best, however, French audiences seeking to see Shakespeare had little opportunity to appreciate him even when presented by Talma, an enthusiastic interpreter.

The most vital elements in the French theatre at this time were, as has been said, undoubtedly the melodrama, along with all the popular forms of entertainment from the eighteenth century; the pantomime, now partially merged with the *pièce à grand spectacle*; the comic opera; and even (in a kind of primitivism) all the cruder forms of the entertainments offered by the fairs. Obviously there was little hope for any

[2]N. Brazier, *Histoire des petits théâtres* (Paris, 1838), pp. 127 ff.

national theatrical revival here. Even when the theatres of the Boulevard did manage to look a little higher for material, it had to be adapted. The theatrical announcements of the Restoration show a profusion of plays based on British sources, especially the novels of Walter Scott. Recognizing also the intense vitality of Shakespeare's work, the purveyors of popular entertainment fell upon his tragedies, in particular, producing transformations of the masterpieces which defy description. *Hamlet* ceased to be the study of a soul and became a tragic pantomime in three acts; *Macbeth*, produced in 1816, emerged as *Les Sorcières d'Ecosse*, a melodrama on the *grand spectacle* pattern centring around the supernatural and with a great deal of violent action added. *The Moor of Venice* we have met already as the *pantomime dialoguée* of Franconi's circus theatre.

Ironically enough, these ill-contrived adaptations at least assured continued attention for the original author. And, whatever their faults might be in French eyes, Shakespeare's plays were vital and genuinely dramatic, whereas the French plays which, for lack of better, cultivated Parisians were obliged to attend, were exceedingly dull. The Théâtre Français, in spite of possessing in Talma one of the greatest of all French actors, and in Mlle Mars a very great actress, was sunk in a morass of mediocrity and boredom. The most dissatisfied among the patrons of the Comédie were precisely those who had seen and heard English drama produced in England. Stendhal, Amédée Pichot and others attacked the classics in their very stronghold, the classic tragedy, which they found tedious in comparison with the vitality of the English plays.

Towards 1827, when these rebels found themselves supported not only by the ardent young Romanticists but also by such moderates as Delécluze and Viollet-le-duc, and by such commanding figures as Charles Nodier and the conservative critic Villemain, it became obvious that any vigorous opposition had largely disappeared. Even political passions had been cooled by the lapse of time and the conciliatory policies of the British Minister, Canning, who constantly advocated friendship with the French liberals. To these more fundamental causes must be added the self-sacrificing persistence of M. Laurent. Finally, by happy coincidence, a French troupe led by Mlle George and Eric Bernard had just finished playing to large and appreciative London audiences. With their chief antagonists in retreat and their friends strong and eager to support them, the English players of 1827 came to a vastly different scene from that faced by their predecessors five years previously. But, although M. Laurent had at last brought his English artists before a Parisian audience, it was still only on sufferance. In a last desperate manœuvre he had obtained the right to alternate with performances at the Odéon only by giving a guarantee of nightly proceeds considerably above the average. None the less, he had at least achieved his ambition; a British troupe was in Paris.

Hailed by enthusiastic if inaccurate press notices (the wrong play was advertised) a composite company from four British theatres opened on September 5 with Sheridan's *The Rivals* and Alingham's *Fortune's Frolic*. Before a full house of sympathetic subscribers, the literary and social *élite* of Paris, William Abbot as director delivered a graceful *compliment d'ouverture* in French. "Even his accent was not displeasing," wrote the *Globe* reviewer on September 11, "since it reminded us that he was a foreigner and that we must be hospitable." The evening went off successfully, although Sheridan's finer touches eluded those not intimately acquainted with English. Two nights later the more pictorial *She Stoops to Conquer* made a happier impression with its greater amount of action and stage business.

On September 11, Charles Kemble's arrival brought the season's first Shakespearean drama, *Hamlet*, a play which made a great though mixed impression on the audience. *Romeo and Juliet*, a play more widely known, was performed next; this presentation profited doubly: first, by contrast with Ducis' inept version and secondly, by the poetic beauty which the audience could sense in many of the scenes. *Othello* followed, but even the cordially inclined still gave it a lukewarm reception; undoubtedly ruthless slashing of the text and a faulty performance by several of the actors contributed to this impression.

During the next fortnight little of a striking nature was attempted; the company gave a group of lighter English comedies and repeated *Romeo and Juliet*, with Abbot replacing Kemble as Romeo and Miss Maria Foote substituting for Harriet Smithson. During this period a move was made to the Théâtre des Italiens, a change favourable for the visitors.

At the Italiens, on October 15, the company gave Rowe's *Jane Shore*, the most favourably received of all their productions. With the exception of three performances of Otway's *Venice Preserved* late in the year, *King Lear* at the opening performance of 1828, and two attempts at *Richard III* in February, the troupe confined themselves until the end of March, 1828, to interpreting light English comedies such as *The Wedding Day*, *Three Weeks after Marriage*, and *Fortune's Frolic*. Sheridan received only three billings and Shakespeare's *The Merchant of Venice* quite failed to please. In the first season, *Jane Shore* had almost as many performances as all the Shakespearean plays combined.

The initial season from September, 1827, until the end of March, 1828, was, then, marked by a series of experiments of varying success. Shakespeare had not made a great impression, had indeed been eclipsed by Rowe. Had the English visit terminated in March, it would have had little more influence than is usually exerted by a *succès d'estime*, Miss Smithson would have been remembered as a graceful and at times compelling actress, Abbot as a sympathetic and generally well received Francophil.

Early in April William Macready arrived in Paris, and Edmund Kean made his début in May; these two great figures of the English stage drew acutely interested audiences, and the effect of their presence was immediately evident. On April 7 and on the following night, Macready gave an impressive performance in *Macbeth*. Later that month he created a sensation in four performances of Knowles' *Virginius*. Then on May 12 the eagerly awaited Kean began a six weeks' series of fourteen performances including *Richard III*, *The Merchant of Venice* on four evenings, *Othello* on three, and *King Lear* on two. Three days after Kean's return to England, Macready appeared again, and in July gave excellent single performances in *Virginius*, *Othello*, and *Jane Shore*, acted twice in *Hamlet*, and scored a resounding triumph in four appearances in Knowles' new version of *William Tell*.

Thus, after eleven months which really embraced two distinct seasons, the first public run of a British company in nineteenth-century Paris came to a close. Early in 1828 the artists had exchanged with the actors of the Comédie Française and of the Théâtre Madame in two benefit performances. Another pleasant variation was a collaboration with the French actor, Doligny, and others in a droll little play *Anglais et Français*. In this production Abbot made several popular appearances in an English-French role. A command performance was also given at Versailles near the beginning of the season.

The company of twenty-five players had given eighty performances. They had presented nearly forty different plays of widely varied nature in spite of inevitable difficulties arising from changing leading performers. The venture had proved a financial success both for the players and for their faithful promoter, Laurent. What had been the results from other points of view?

II

Although the constant demand of the Anglophil enthusiasts had been for Shakespeare, they did not hear a great amount of his work in comparison with the number of other plays presented. The reasons for this were various. The limitation of the company's numbers prevented the staging of such plays as *The Merchant of Venice* and *Richard III* except by ruthless elimination of characters. In some cases the difficulty was the leading actor, for instance, when the troupe waited for Kemble or for Macready.

Chief among the causes of the limited presentation of Shakespeare was the fact that the Parisians frequently found his works almost overpowering and greeted them with such restrained enthusiasm as to discourage repetitions. The *Globe* critic, discussing the elements in *Hamlet* foreign to French taste and tradition, wrote on September 15: "It contains what might well shock the public if the public had not sensed under these exterior forms and events a genuine beauty and the development of a highly dramatic soul." During the first season no Shakespeare play except *Romeo and Juliet* was performed more than twice, and Miss Foote's special appearance as Juliet accounted for the additional offering of that play. The audience had eagerly anticipated this play, and did enjoy certain poetic passages, but the French seemed to find a great deal of it beyond their comprehension. Although admitting that "this succession of images so true to life and so tragic produced an inexpressible emotion in everyone present," the critic for the *Globe* on September 15 described the play as having been presented "with very mixed success."

Two performances of *Othello* near the beginning of the first season convinced both audience and actors that *The Moor of Venice* was not to their taste. Kean was able to perform the role on three occasions, and Macready only once at the very close of the season.

Terry's single performance in *King Lear* proved such a disappointment that the play was dropped by the Abbot troupe, although Kean later gave two performances. The ever-benevolent *Globe*, however, mustered a kind word for the first effort, writing on January 12: "How much better we grasp Shakespeare's conception after this performance, how much more we will enjoy reading the complete play as we recall Miss Smithson and Mr. Terry." Kean made a better impression in the play if for a rather dubious reason. Writing in *L'Incorruptible* on June 8, Saint Eloy somewhat ingenuously suggested that Kean's physical debility made him peculiarly fitted to present the aged and weakened Lear. It is noteworthy that the tragic ending eschewed by many eighteenth-century producers was chosen for presentation in Paris. This version would certainly prove more acceptable to French audiences than the fatuous adaptations often given in England even at this time.

During his six-week visit, Kean naturally displayed his talents in a wide variety of roles. *Richard III*, in which he had created such an impression in England, had little effect in Paris except to underline the actor's premature decline especially because this play centres so markedly on the main character. But, in spite of his decline, Kean was still an actor who could on occasion lift a play to great heights. Recalling the visit of 1827-8, the veteran critic Delécluze remarked in his *Souvenirs*: "Seeing Shakespeare's plays staged carefully at Paris by Kean, Macready, Kemble, and Miss Smithson one momentarily forgot the essential nature of the French theatre and allowed oneself to be genuinely moved by the gigantic scaffolding of these dramas."[3] Kean's triumph as Shylock contrasted sharply with Terry's slight success in the part in January, when the play had been given twice. Quite aside from the interpretation, the critics were almost unanimously severe in their comments on it; to them it seemed a strange mixture of drama, comedy and farce.

Macready was counted on for a brilliant interpretation of Macbeth and he opened his performances in France in that role. Although he performed splendidly, the play was given only twice more, once the next evening and again later. The grisly mixture of the witches' brew evoked mingled laughter and disgust, while the savage and violent

---

[3]Cited by Eric Partridge, *The French Romantics' Knowledge of English Literature (1820-1848)* (Paris, 1924), p. 209.

nature of the intrigue came too close to melodrama to satisfy the audience. Miss Smithson was inadequate as Lady Macbeth; and the modest run of the play was due only to Macready.

During the first season *Hamlet* appeared on the bills five times at long intervals, with Kemble and Abbot playing the Prince. The popularity of the tragedy was patently owing to Miss Smithson's appealing delineation of Ophelia. During Macready's final series in July, *Hamlet* appeared twice more, still with the same actress as Ophelia.

The productions of Shakespeare's works amounted to just over 20 items of the 110 performances given. This proportion might seem reasonably impressive but it has also to be noted that a single play, *Jane Shore*, was presented a dozen times during the entire season and was chosen for the July farewell benefit performance. Why should this play, for which no literary claims can be made, have proved so popular with the French? Even the French reviewers do not explain the matter but the many romantic elements in the play may offer a clue.

Virginius and *William Tell* had enjoyed a moderate London run but were very successful in Paris. Again we are puzzled as to the cause of such warm receptions; *William Tell*, in particular, a pedestrian and confused rehandling of Schiller's drama, retained little of the German masterpiece. The critics, however, put the playwright in his proper place while admiring the interpreter. On July 6 the critic of *L'Incorruptible* remarked: "The new English tragedy is neither better nor worse than the hundred tragedies on this subject which have been hissed or applauded during the last forty years in England; but it has over the others an immense advantage, that of having in its leading role one of the greatest actors to grace the modern stage."

The physical conditions under which the players strove to produce Shakespeare did not determine the reception, but undoubtedly are a partial explanation of a reduced effect. Both stages, particularly that of the Italiens, lacked the dimensions necessary for the proper staging of Shakespeare's epic conceptions, and the furnishings and scenery were inadequate. Since a nineteenth-century audience had moved very far away from the Elizabethan theatre's method of handling "the vasty fields of France," the English troupe had to try to give some suggestion of setting but their décor was inadequate and incongruous, and the inappropriate reappearances of certain details of it shocked everyone. The actors fared better in the matter of costumes. They had some of their own wardrobes and profited also from the ignorance of audiences to whom historical accuracy in dress was still a relative novelty. None the less, in April, 1828, the critic of *La Pandore*, after complimenting the company on certain improvements in scenery, continued somewhat smugly: "But let the English actors please remember that in England they are far from having reached the perfection that we display in the costumes and settings of a drama."

The exigencies of casting were detrimental to certain plays. It was not until Macready and Kean arrived that the great dramas could be adequately presented; and, quite aside from the question of quality, there arose the embarrassment of limited numbers, especially in a foreign country where Abbot could not easily enlist extra players. *Richard III* suffered particularly and *Hamlet* lost a round dozen lesser characters including one of the grave-diggers. *Macbeth* lost several secondary personages among the lords and even Lady Macduff. In *Lear* the French king disappeared and, more surprisingly, so did the fool; *The Merchant of Venice* sacrificed two of Portia's suitors and two servants. Necessary as these deletions may have appeared to Abbot, they could scarcely have added to the appeal of the plays, except for a doubtful exception in Lear's fool, who would probably have proved even more incomprehensible than Launcelot Gobbo.

Most formidable of all the forces which hindered a French appreciation of Shakespeare must be held the atrocious textual maltreatment of the plays presented in Paris. The ruthless and fatuous adaptations of the eighteenth century still held the stage at that time in London and it was these which were too often given by the visitors to Paris. *Romeo and Juliet* also suffered from the ignominy of Garrick's ending. To facilitate the enjoyment of the plays, the company published special editions and these give us the exact versions used on the opening nights by the French audiences. In Cibber's version of *Richard III*, Shakespeare's combined study and chronicle became a simple portrait of the king, with rearrangements, abridgements, and, worse still, additions by Cibber and Garrick. *King Lear*, after Nahum Tate and John Kemble had cut, grafted, and polished it wavered between a tragic and a happy ending. Although the Abbot company usually gave the former ending, it was little more than a distorted shadow of the original. That Shakespeare made any impression whatever in such circumstances bears further tribute to his unquenchable vitality.

Certain special textual distortions in addition were necessary in Paris. Here we may at least partially exculpate the actors. The censorship, though less stupid and severe than in Penley's times, deprecated the representation of royalty or the clergy on the stage, and demanded the omission of a good many lusty Elizabethan terms. To this must be added the unofficial but equally rigorous and powerful censorship of French public taste with its theatrical code of *les bienséances*. When one considers that further deletions were sometimes made to allow the staging of another play on the same evening, it is surprising that Shakespearean drama survived at all. The plays, as presented by Abbot, were reduced by one-quarter or even one-half of their original length.

The comedies present an entirely different picture from that of the dramas. The French did not await them with much anticipation, firmly believing that the English had nothing to teach them in the field of comedy, either in the matter and style of the plays or in their presentation. Nor did the English visit do much to alter their belief.

The distribution of the comedies in the two seasons reveals the significant fact that, while the regular company was playing from October to March, it attempted to catch public fancy with comedies of various types, but when the great interpreters of drama were available little place remained for comedy. In the case of the Kean-Macready seasons, the brief visits of the artists demanded roles worthy of their stature. None the less, it does seem striking that, aside from Kean's magnificent production of *The Merchant of Venice*, only three comedies were given, one of which was the completely new presentation, Massinger's *A New Way to Pay Old Debts*, in which Kean appeared twice. Macready confined himself strictly to tragic and dramatic roles.

The nature of the plays is also revealing. The classic English comedies were least appreciated, *The Rivals* and *She Stoops to Conquer* appearing but once each, while *The School for Scandal* reached only the second performance. More popular was the farcical group on the marriage theme. Once again the influence of the leading player was evident; the frequent billing of Mrs. Cowley's play *The Weather Cock* was largely owing to the capacities of Maria Foote who, in her fortnight's visit, acted in this piece four times.

Most of the comedies belonged to a special category, that of translations and adaptations into English from the French. *Love, Law and Physic, The Irish Tutor, Plot and Counter Plot, A Roland for an Oliver*, and *Simpson and Co.* all were borrowed from Scribe, Picard, and other French dramatists. The sources apparently were not indicated because they were so obvious but were scrupulously noted by the French critics. Naturally this group did not appeal much to audiences familiar with the original versions. Their interest lay only in the opportunity which they afforded for observing the results of adaptation for foreign consumption. Yet this process was not really being fully carried out since the adaptations were being made with presentation to a French rather than an English audience in mind. The comical mixture, *Anglais et Français*, was always given under special circumstances such as a benefit. Its principal feature was the bilingual antics of Mr. Abbot and it had no special literary significance.

Apparently the basic difficulty was that of language. We most fully realize our deficiencies in a foreign tongue by listening to comedy in its idiom. All the cordiality of the Anglophils in 1827 could not give them the capacity to savour the subtleties of Sheridan and his fellows. There was probably much truth in the squib launched by the *Courrier des théâtres* at the two elements in the audience—the French and the English—at the opening play. "*The Rivals* was looked at by the one and understood by the other with equal satisfaction."

It might be, indeed, that the English comedies were presented chiefly as a bid for the patronage of the English in Paris, who could enjoy them until the arrival of Kean and Macready drew the French to hear Shakespeare. The occasional combined programmes with the troupe of the Opéra Italien, whose hall the English players shared, also suggests an attempt to gain popular appeal.

The one Shakespearean comedy, *The Merchant of Venice*, introduced entirely new difficulties. Here the profound difference between French and English tastes made comprehension and appreciation virtually impossible. To French minds *The Merchant of Venice* appeared a grotesque hodge-podge of sentimentality, buffoonery, horror and cruelty; and Terry's performance further contributed to the failure of the comedy. Kean's interpretation of Shylock left a much more powerful and just impression on the audience; but in its truncated form, lacking a commanding Portia, and being essentially an imaginative type of comedy which the French did not understand, the effect of the play as a whole amounted to a failure.

The actors' interpretations of their roles also affected the reception of the plays although the British characteristics were less obvious in comedy than in drama or tragedy. Liston, the chief comic actor of the troupe, was a mature and highly regarded comedian. He stood in English public opinion on a level with Mathews, and like Mathews was compared by the French to Potier and Brunet. These comparisons suggest that Liston was rather a portrayer of the exaggerated and idiosyncratic than an interpreter of sophisticated comedy. Yet his first impression on Paris indicates that he may have curbed his whimsical tendencies. Comparing him to Baptiste *cadet*, the *Globe* on September 11, 1827, suggested that Liston was simply playing himself. "Everything about him is natural and easy, his animation is controlled; he disdains caricature." Even more successful was Tyrone Power, whose vigour and sparkle immediately caught the eye of the Parisians. "As Sir Lucius O'Trigger," wrote Porel and Monval, "Mr. Power appeared as a highly comic actor; the vivacity of his delivery, the mobility of his face, his infectious zest put him in the first rank."[4] The other male actors in the comedies were scarcely more than utility figures.

The feminine comedy roles were played by Harriet Smithson and the brief visitor, Maria Foote. Miss Smithson's appeal in Paris quickly proved to be in the pitiable emotional roles of Jane Shore, Ophelia, Juliet, and Desdemona. She had little more than her graceful beauty to recommend her in comedy, although one critic remarked on her Portia, commenting that her wit, grace, vivacity and power affected him even more because, pantomime not availaing in this case, she rose to the occasion by splendid declamation. Miss Foote, a thoroughly spirited actress, suffered somewhat from comparison with a rival who had already gained the sympathies of the Parisians. On the whole, she availed herself of good vehicles particularly suited to her talents; and although *The School for Scandal* received generally unfavourable notices, Miss Foote was praised as having "delightfully depicted the grace, cunning and flightiness of Sir Peter's better half." In *The Weather Cock* she scintillated; in *Romeo and Juliet* she astonished the audience by her deeper capabilities. "This charming actress agreeably surprised us by her talent in tragedy," the *Globe* admitted. "She left the victory wavering between Miss Smithson and herself." Yet, in

[4]Paul Porel et G. Monval, *L'Odeon: Histoire administrative anecdotique et littéraire du second théâtre français (1818–53)* (Paris, 1882), p. 98.

spite of all this, her visit still left the critics somewhat puzzled to explain her success in London.

It seems clear that in content, style, and interpretation no great impression was made by the comedies. M. Saint Eloy of *L'Incorruptible* sums up the matter in his article of May 4: "If there had been three times as many present the hall would still not have been full. This indifference on the part of the public, more than all our arguments, should convince the English actors that they will make no impression here with comedy."

If the interpretation of the comedies did not evoke much reaction from the critics, that of the dramas did, the more so because the actors were much more interesting.

The first of the leading Shakespearean actors, Charles Kemble, made a considerable impression in *Hamlet* although, to judge from the critics, the impact of the play almost exceeded that of its interpreters. In *Romeo and Juliet* the balcony scene won favourable comment for both of the chief characters in the play. "We have never perhaps seen more convincing grief on the stage," wrote the *Globe* of Kemble as Romeo. In his final role as Othello, Kemble did not greatly excite the admiration of his audience, leaving the impression of a phlegmatic Englishman rather than of a passionate Moor. In his brief sojourn he barely sustained his advance reputation; even his declamations, which might have won him favour in France, were ridiculously exaggerated and provoked unfavourable comment, especially among his English hearers. The French critics compared him with Talma and found him lacking in Talma's brilliance of tragic inspiration and profundity, although they did concede him a certain ease of gesture and deportment. These they found distinctively English and effective in giving increased vivacity and flexibility to a play. The *Courrier des théâtres* noted on September 28: "Mr. Charles Kemble has said farewell. We are far from recognizing in this actor the *extraordinary* talent so graciously attributed to him."

Abbot, the only other leading masculine figure in the initial season, owed his popularity to a combination of geniality and moderate capacity, and to his obvious efforts to please the French public. His chief triumphs were in the comedies early in the season in which he played opposite Miss Foote, although he received generally favourable notices throughout the winter in such secondary roles as Macduff or Edgar in *Lear*.

Kean's visit, in spite of striking moments, left the audiences with the impression that they had viewed the wreck of a great actor rather than the artist himself. Even at forty Kean's physical powers were heavily ravaged by hardships and excesses; his voice especially had suffered. In England, he had maintained an uneasy popularity by the flashing genius which he could at times display in the tragic Shakespearean roles. In Paris, his remarkable powers of characterization and pantomime coupled with the occasional extraordinary effects which he could achieve with a glance, at least suggested to the reviewers what the actor must have been at his best. The moderate critics wavered in their judgments on Kean as Othello. The *Globe* felt that Kean really did not bring the role to life until late in the play. *L'Incorruptible* found that Kean's final performance in *Othello* justified his reputation as a great actor. But his rough and careless delivery alienated even those to whom the language was not familiar, and his grim accentuation of Othello's ferocity especially marred the role for French listeners. Only in *The Merchant of Venice* did he really arouse the admiration of his audience, a feat the more notable because the play had been coldly received earlier in the winter. In fact, its popularity with Kean was such that other plays or repeat performances which Kean had planned were replaced by Shylock. "At last we have seen Kean," wrote the *Globe*, "Kean in all the beauty, all the fullness of his talent . . . . His interpretation was as alive, as poetic, as powerful as his conception of the role." The singleness of Kean's Shylock, nursing his hatred, redeemed the play for the Parisians; his rehabilitation of the comedy for French minds furnished much material for all the reviewers. *La Pandore* commented on May 26: "The role of Shylock, a profound conception of Shakespeare, completely suits Kean's talents . . . his bitter sarcasm, convulsive laugh, and fiery glances, the fierce anticipation as he whets his knife, his piteous exit, called forth frequent applause." "Kean has finally vindicated himself," we read in *L'Incorruptible*, also on May 26; "the first presentation of *The Merchant of Venice* was a triumph for him . . . Kean in fact showed himself worthy of his great reputation in the satanic role of the Jew, Shylock."

The actor who truly established his reputation in France at this time was William Macready. His sonorous voice and his variety of style from tender intimacy in *Virginius* and *William Tell* to awful grandeur in *Macbeth* and *Othello* appeared even more admirable to the public and reviewers because nature had refused him other qualities usually associated with a tragic actor. In *Macbeth* particularly his fiery handling of the role carried even the objectionable portions of the play and left an impression of epic fierceness. Except in *Hamlet*, where his tender and sentimental interpretation of the prince failed to please, Macready received the warmest of receptions. Of his Othello the *Globe* wrote: "It is impossible to bring out more skilfully all the nuances of that character at once so violent and so tender, or better to link love with fury, strength with weakness, or the energy of crime with the listlessness of remorse." Macready's crowning triumphs came in two lesser plays by Knowles, *Virginius* and *William Tell*. In discussing the former, *La Pandore* paid special tribute to him: "How often during this tragedy the actor transmitted to the audience the keen emotions which his soul seemed to feel!" In his analysis of *William Tell*, the critic for the *Globe* suggested that this second-rate play had really been carried by Macready. "We may justly attribute the greater part of its success to the immense talent of the actor carrying the role of Tell, to which all the other roles are subordinated." One inevitably recalls the comments on Kean in *Richard III* where the burden of a similarly dominant role had proved too much for the enfeebled actor. Contrasts between Kean and his younger rival were inevitable. Having evaluated the work of the older actor the critic of *L'Incorruptible* continued: "But his rival seems to me as much above him as nature is above studied art, as strength is above exhaustion." Other critics paid the younger English actor sincere compliments on what they felt to be his kinship with, and indeed imitation of, Talma. Such an artist they could offer as a model for young French actors and as an incitement to greater effort.

The *Mercure de France* well expresses the general reaction: "Macready and Mme Malibran are the sensations of the day ... In *Macbeth* and especially in *Virginius* ... Macready has displayed truly admirable talent." The visitor even received the wry but definite compliment of being rivalled by a burlesque version of *Virginius* presented at the Théâtre de la Gaîté. In his own right, as well as in contrast with the other chief actors who appeared, Macready undoubtedly carried off the laurels in Paris.

Harriet Smithson, the one actress who caught and held public favour throughout the winter, may almost be said to have saved the entire venture. A favourite from the beginning for her charm and beauty, Miss Smithson steadily enhanced her reputation as a tragic actress in the roles of Jane Shore, Juliet, Desdemona, and Ophelia. In this last part, which the French found so difficult to understand, her wistful tenderness particularly won applause and comprehension. Harriet Smithson's career in London had been discouragingly obscure and her Irish accent was accounted an insuperable obstacle to success; the Parisians exulted over the sweet melody of her voice and found no offense in her Irish brogue.

Miss Smithson undoubtedly kept the English company in favour throughout the early months of 1828. She supported Kean and Macready in the tragedies which they presented, but her weakness in heavy tragic roles revealed itself most clearly when she played Lady Macbeth (luckily this was not often). At her benefit performance in March, 1828, the stage lay buried in flowers, she received impressive gifts from the royal family and civil authorities, and Abbot's tribute to her as the mainstay of the troupe was repeatedly "drowned in applause."

III

What were the results of this remarkable display of *bonne entente*? The literary influence of the English visit is so intertwined with the history of the Romantic period in France that any attempt to deal with it presents the danger of becoming involved in the complicated history of French literature during the late twenties and throughout the thirties. However, a number of relatively non-controversial comments may be made.[5]

Little need be said of such convinced *cosmopolites* and Anglophils as Nodier, Stendhal, or Pichot. For these the arrival of Shakespearean drama was the joyful culmination of many hopes and efforts. Since their comprehension and appreciation were relatively complete, their pleasure was keen. No great change in attitude or in literature would be expected from such figures. One naturally asks if any wavering minds were swept into the Romantic fold by this particular foreign influence but it would be rash to suggest that an influence so specific and limited was the determining one in any literary career. All French literature was in flux at that moment. The battles of 1827 to 1830 raged

---

[5]Those wishing to consult an exhaustive treatment of English literary influence in France at this period are referred to the extremely detailed work of Eric Partridge: *The French Romantics' Knowledge of English Literature (1820–1848)*.

on the dramatic front but the position of the Romantic novel was also being confirmed and both Lamartine and Musset published significant volumes of poetry in 1829 and 1830.

The literary classicists remained unmoved and reaped their reward of oblivion. A small group which might be called the compromisers attempted unsuccessfully to add a few exterior trappings to the Alexandrine tragedy. The more timid Romantics with their modest prose versions of historical dramas were eclipsed by the fiery young poets of the avant-garde. The group on which the strongest and most telling influence prevailed, that is, the critics, were not in the main creative writers. Therefore, one must look among the small group of coming dramatic poets for any concrete results.

A number of the leading Romantic figures were at critical points in their careers at that moment. It can be argued that the stimulation of the English dramas exerted some influence upon a number of them, an influence, however, which varied greatly in nature and immediacy.

When the British artists opened their season Hugo was busy writing a manifesto in his preface to *Cromwell*. The inclusion of Shakespeare among the examples in this may well reflect a special interest in the company's presence. The broader effect on Hugo seems more apparent in his later plays. Hugo's knowledge of English did not permit him to follow the plays with textual comprehension, and he obviously failed to appreciate Shakespeare's subtle psychology, but he did receive a powerful incentive to use the imaginative pictorial and social approach to history. His contact with Shakespeare probably strengthened Hugo's inherent tendencies in the drama, and may well have changed his emphasis. Hugo's tendency towards the melodramatic would certainly seem more justified in his own mind if he had the example of Shakespeare to support it. And the historical approach, distorted somewhat by Hugo's own special conceptions, had abundant examples in Shakespeare.

Alexandre Dumas loudly proclaimed his debt to playwright and players and unreservedly attributed his determination for a career in drama to them. His statements are confirmed by the Romantic dramas which he produced between 1829 and 1836. Dumas, even more than Hugo, caught and reproduced the spirit and fierce power of English historical drama. The ardent disciples of Shakespeare carried the tendencies which they believed they saw in his work to romantic extremes. The physical violence, the superabundance of episode, the threats and rantings of *Henri III et sa cour* or of *La Tour de Nesle* are more than a mere continuation of the Empire melodrama. They are the melodrama plus Shakespeare plus Dumas, a strange and powerful mixture. Delacroix writes of the author: "Poor Dumas, whom I really like, and who probably thinks himself a second Shakespeare, does not leave in our minds either clear details or a unity of impression. The elements of his plays are not judiciously balanced."[6]

One specific outcome of Kean's visit remains in Dumas' sombre play, *Kean, ou génie et désordre*, produced in 1836. Here the French dramatist, without entering into delicate analysis, outlined the tragic story of Kean's mingled powers and weaknesses presenting a gripping picture of a genius cursed by his own nature. While most of the anecdotes concerning Kean's behaviour in 1828 may be dismissed as fabrications, there is no doubt that his performances on and off the Paris stage furnished the author with abundant inspiration.

Vigny's case tends to be somewhat deceptive. His admiration for and imitation of Scott, his assiduous frequenting of Romantic *cénacles*, his English marriage, and his dramatic leanings might well suggest to us that he too would be a passionate disciple of Shakespeare. This would be further encouraged by his translation of *Romeo and Juliet* in collaboration with Emile Deschamps in 1828. Finally, there was his version of *Othello*, played in 1829. The examination of a few facts, however, seems to prove that Vigny was never swept away by the English dramatist. He warns us that *Othello* is simply a scrupulous translation of the English text, without committing himself about the play. His own dramas are scarcely in the Shakespearean mould; *Chatterton*, with its factitious English setting, is a *pièce à thèse* and his other plays fall into the French tradition.

In spite of his youth, Musset had already made his entry into the Romantic circles and he had attended the plays. It is customary to attribute the distinctive form of Musset's comedies, with their imaginative, exotic, fairy-like settings, to the fact that he wrote closet dramas rather than stage plays. His whimsical yet serious playing with ideas he drew, according to tradition, from the eighteenth-century playwright Marivaux. Yet a case can be made for the hypothesis that Shakespeare influenced Musset in both setting and philosophy. The multiple

[6] *Journal d'Eugène Delacroix, édité par André Joubin* (Paris, 1932; 3 vols.), I, p. 324.

scenes called for by the English dramatist were made all too apparent to Musset and everyone else by the pitifully inadequate sets of the Odéon and the Italiens. The whimsical playing with ideas so apparent in the clowns of Shakespeare certainly has its counterpart in the gay or pensive comments of similar personages of Musset in such comedies as *Fantasio, Carmosine,* and *Un Caprice.* And from the Shakespearean chronicles Musset could draw his *André del Sarto* or his sombre and powerful historical tragedy *Lorenzaccio.*

As well as influencing the younger writers, the English visit left its mark on French actors, on the critics, and on the public. The younger members of the Théâtre Français and other theatres frequently attended the Odéon and the Italiens. They quickly recognized the profound difference between the artificial delivery of the French and the realistic, at times terrifyingly realistic, English presentations. Making allowance for the nature of the dramas being interpreted, they still were forced to recognize the superiority of their British rivals. In moments of fierce intensity of emotion, the dishevelled hair, disordered garments, and even contorted postures of the actors and actresses alike profoundly impressed their French colleagues. This was particularly true with Kean, who in such roles as Richard III and Shylock filled his audiences with dismay and horror by his vivid representations of despair and malevolence.

The depiction of physical violence and physical pain, largely banished from the French stage, came as a thunderbolt to actors accustomed to experiencing these only in description. The players' reactions to these stimuli equally impressed the French; Miss Smithson's real tears made the perfunctory gesturing of her French counterparts seem absurd. The French continued to apply the term *boucherie* to some of the violence, but there was undoubtedly a more forceful approach on the Paris stage after 1827. An English innovation greatly admired was the sardonic sneer by which the men expressed disdain or concealed mental anguish. Repeated mention of this theatrical device and Hugo's frequent use of it reveal the impression which it made on the French.

Most impressive in all the English realism, the representations of madness and death created a furore among authors, actors, and audiences. Miss Smithson's Ophelia became a public figure in Paris, while the profusion of death scenes, which originally horrified Parisians, ultimately became the vogue, famliar to all students of French Romantic drama. The temptation to act in the English style would certainly be accentuated by the number of adaptations from Shakespeare then being given in Paris. The repertoires of the following seasons were thickly sown with performances of Shakespeare in various French versions, most of them improvements over those of ten years previously. In an *Almanach théâtral* for 1829 we read: "During November Shakespeare has invaded several Paris theatres; sometimes on the same day there have been given *The Moor of Venice* at the Comédie Française, *Othello* at the Opéra Comique, *Macbeth* at the Odéon and at the Porte-Saint-Martin."

The pantomime of the British actors aroused not only the admiration of their French colleagues but also imitation, sometimes slavishly careful, sometimes highly exaggerated. The English players naturally used every possible resource of pantomime, gesture, and expression to aid those whose understanding of English remained weak. Naturally, too, some French imitators further magnified this already over-drawn performance.

The reactions of the critics are the most interesting study. The intransigent nationalists, led by the *Courrier des théâtres*, maintained their hostility without noticeable wavering, deplored the presence of foreign actors in a crowded theatrical field, resented their attempt to teach anything to Frenchmen, viewed with alarm the invasion of the French stage by Shakespeare, and, in general, gave in 1827 the same examples of wilful prejudice as in 1822. The only difference between the reactions of the two dates lay in the much smaller proportion and influence of the die-hard opposition.

The opposite camp, best represented by *Le Globe*, after long clamouring for English drama, hailed its arrival and continuance with great satisfaction. Their pleasure, however, did not lull their critical faculties when the extravagances of English drama provoked their sensibilities. Even good will could not reconcile them to parts of *Lear* and *Othello*, or to some features of *The Merchant of Venice*. The moderate group, represented by *La Pandore*, illustrated a fairly general tendency of gradual approval even of a play initially disliked. Obviously this veering of opinion had a variety of causes. On occasion the more favourable verdict came simply from greater familiarity and fuller comprehension. At times the modification of action and speech by the players sufficed to alter a reviewer's reactions. With *The Merchant of*

Venice and *Othello*, a change of actor put the play in quite a different light. In general, the judicious critics progressed towards a more favourable view of English drama, usually for valid reasons, while maintaining that critical integrity on which the French pride themselves.

The artistic repercussions of the visit inevitably linked themselves with the general movement of Romanticism. Among the painters the first and most indisputable reaction was that of Boulanger and Deveria. Although no particular artistic merits may be claimed by their work, it has both interest and historic value. During the season Deveria joined with Boulanger to produce an album of the chief actors and roles: *Souvenirs du théâtre anglais à Paris* with commentary by Moreau. The volume remains a most valuable source of information on the visit itself and the French reactions to it.

Delacroix, who represents Romanticism chiefly in the field of painting, felt naturally attracted to Shakespeare, although the precise influence of the visit would be difficult to specify. Of a poetic nature, Delacroix especially enjoyed drama and, when in London in 1825, divided his admiration between the new English painting which he keenly appreciated, and the theatre which he attended assiduously. In September, 1827, he wrote: "The English have begun their season. They are now the style.... The most stubborn classics are yielding. The consequences of this innovation are incalculable."[7] In 1828 he followed the performances of both Kean and Macready. Delacroix was doubly attracted to Shakespeare. In the first instance, the weird, the grotesque, the florid, and the melodramatic elements of the English dramatist appealed strongly to him. Secondly, an author such as Shakespeare appealed to the literary side of Delacroix who in many of his paintings shows himself the interpretive illustrator of Dante, Tasso, Cervantes, Byron, and Shakespeare. Actually, the pictures in which Shakespeare's characters appear were painted considerably later. "Hamlet with the skull of Yorick" dates from 1839, "Romeo's Farewell" from the forties. It is interesting to find in his journal under date of December 29, 1860, a large group of proposed subjects for paintings inspired by *Romeo and Juliet* and other plays of Shakespeare; a number of these were executed.[8] Increasingly numerous entries in his later

[7] Eugène Delacroix, *Lettres*, ed. Burty (Paris, 1878), I, under September 26, 1827.
[8] *Journal d'Eugène Delacriox*, III, pp. 313-16.

journals demonstrate that the spirit of Shakespeare continued to attract him, indeed haunted him. Under date of February, 1847, he wrote:

Grenier came to do a pastel study . . . we discussed Mozart and Beethoven. He found in Beethoven a strain of misanthropy and despair not matched by the others. We compared him with Shakespeare. Grenier did me the honour of ranging me in the same category as these stern contemplators of human nature.[9]

But Delacroix, in spite of his admiration for Shakespeare, whom he regarded as a kind of Michaelangelo of the drama, still could write in April, 1849, "We will never be Shakespeareans."

The opposite of Delacroix in many ways but, like him, intensely interested in English history at this time, Delaroche may well have seized this opportunity to gain direct contact with the history and legend of Britain. His celebrated "Death of Queen Elizabeth" dates from 1827 and "The Princes in the Tower" from 1830, suggesting a preoccupation with subjects which might well have been inspired by the English visitors. We discover also that during Macready's visit in 1844, Delaroche enjoyed repeated contacts with the great actor.

The most profoundly affected of all the artistic group, the composer Berlioz, will be familiar to all students of this period. His passionate devotion to the works of Shakespeare and to Miss Smithson may be gathered from his own and other writings.[10] There is no doubt that Shakespeare exerted great influence upon the spirit and work of this most romantic of all musicians. It may seem surprising that Berlioz did not use more of his plays as direct inspiration for compositions, but the explanation surely lies in the fact that Berlioz was not really an operatic composer. The debatable case, his *Damnation de Faust*, is strictly a dramatic symphony, barely able to sustain interest in presentation. But in his own way, he utilized a number of Shakespearean works. He began the overture to *King Lear* during his stay in Rome and completed it in 1831; in 1833 he attempted to work on *Much Ado about Nothing*, although it was over thirty years later that he completed it as a two-act comic opera *Béatrice et Bénédict*. His *Fantaisie dramatique* based on *The Tempest* dates from 1834, the dramatic symphony, *Roméo et Juliette*, from 1838. And by sombre coincidence his

[9] *Ibid.*, I, p.194.
[10] Hector Berlioz, *Mémoires* (Paris, 1870), *passim*. Also, Hector Berlioz, *Lettres intimes, avec une préface par Charles Gounod* (Paris, 1882), *passim*.

Mort d'Ophelia appeared in 1854, the year in which Harriet Smithson, who had been to the Parisians *la belle Ophelia*, died in sorrow and exile. Berlioz never ceased to hold Shakespeare in a veneration which approached idolatry, and to follow in his wild fashion what he thought were Shakespeare's tenets of life.

9 · Anticlimax

At the close of their Paris season in July the Abbot troupe decided to attempt a number of provincial appearances. Accordingly, they visited Rouen in August to give five performances. At the opening Abbot's compliment in French came with special grace as invoking the good will of his hearers he paid his respects to their illustrious fellow citizen Corneille, "the father of French tragedy." The company opened with *Jane Shore*, the most popular play of their winter season. From Shakespeare they gave *Romeo and Juliet* and *Hamlet*; the other tragedy was *Venice Preserved*. The comedies included two of the marriage farces and the mixed production, *Anglais et Français*, in which Abbot collaborated with several actors from the Rouen Théâtre des Arts. All these plays were well patronized and cordially received.[1]

The following month the company presented its standard repertoire in Le Havre. During this visit, Miss Smithson received an offer to play in Covent Garden, a proposition which she unwisely refused. Back in Paris the players gave two performances before visiting Bordeaux. Here the troupe encountered such ill fortune that it disbanded, and the majority of the players made their way back to England with considerable difficulty. Certain members did return to Paris, Abbot and Miss Smithson making fleeting appearances there throughout the winter. At the beginning of March, 1829, for example, the two appeared in scenes from *Romeo and Juliet* at a benefit for the French actor Huet. Soon after this performance Miss Smithson left Paris and, after a brief journey to Holland, returned to England. There she spent the next year, partly in London, partly on tour. Not until early in 1830 is there any further trace of her in France.

Meanwhile a second Paris visit had been attempted by an English troupe; this was much briefer and consequently made slighter impact. On July 23, 1829, a small Drury Lane company, headed by James

---

[1] J. E. Bouteiller, *Histoire complète et méthodique des théâtres de Rouen* (Rouen, 1860–80; 4 vols.), III, pp. 355 ff.

Wallack and with Mrs. West as leading lady, opened at the Théâtre Italien. Wallack came of a theatrical family, his father having been a member of Philip Astley's company. From childhood, when he had made his début in London pantomime, he played a wide variety of secondary roles in the capital, the provinces, and even America, and held the post of stage manager at Drury Lane. Although he was a disciple of the dignified elder Kemble, he himself excelled in melodrama, the contradiction arising from a lack of sympathy in his own nature which made him inadequate in genuinely tragic roles. Mrs. West had played many supporting characters in London in both comic and tragic parts. It was generally admitted, however, that she lacked the intensity required in tragic heroines, and, as her humorous delineations were unconvincing, her only excellence lay in tender roles. In these she did possess considerable appeal. Thus, the public were invited to enjoy a pale copy of what they had seen the previous year. The only familiar figure of any significance was William Abbot, who again was stage manager and took some secondary roles. A few minor members of the 1828 company also reappeared.

The troupe planned a limited number of performances. The list of eight advertised suggests that Abbot had learned from experience that a lengthy run in Paris required the stimulus of great names. The series of less than three weeks included only six appearances and offered seven different items. Three of these, Sheridan's adaptation of Kotzebue's *Pizarro*, an adaptation of Shakespeare's *Coriolanus*, and that standby of the English stage, *Douglas*, were new to the Parisian public. *Jane Shore*, *The Stranger*, *The Merchant of Venice*, and *The Day after the Wedding* had all been given by the Abbot-Smithson players.

Without journalistic notice, great reputation, or official patronage to help him, Wallack opened with the drama *Pizarro* before a small and apathetic audience. The critics, to whom English players were now far from a novelty, first directed their attention to the play and Sheridan's version received very sharp treatment. French political tension, soon to explode in revolution, created acute sensitivity to political content in plays; *Pizarro* impressed the critics as out-of-date propaganda, while the melodramatic intrigue precluded any subtle interpretation by the actors. The *Globe* regretted the lack of scope for Wallack and remarked: "his pantomime [is] at times expressive, although generally too formal." *La Pandore* in a moderately lengthy treatment of the actor's performance, declared its preference for Wallack over a wheezing and exhausted Kean but placed him far below Macready. The death of the hero in the play provoked an ironic comment on Wallack's particular handling of the incident: "He seems to have the talent of dying handsomely and of falling full length; a merit highly appreciated by our neighbours but which we admire much less." Mrs. West fared worse with both audience and critics. *La Pandore* reported: "Mrs. West was less graciously received than her companion. Her pleasant but vacuous features, her lack of naturalness and sensitivity, her artificial appeal were severely judged." The critic suggested that cold silence in the face of Mrs. West's simperings would have been a more suitable expression of disapproval than the hissings indulged in by some members of the audience.

Othello still exercised a kind of horrible fascination for the Parisian public, and drew a much larger audience. Here, however, Wallack floundered out of his depth, and it was Mrs. West, in a more suitable part, who received favourable mention. Her most appealing roles were precisely those which, like Desdemona, demand tenderness and resignation. The critics, however, nostalgically recalled the more lofty interpretations of Kean and Miss Smithson.

The third presentation, Shakespeare's *Coriolanus*, afforded Wallack his chief opportunity to impress the public. *Coriolanus* was a type of Shakespearean play new to the French and one which encroached on the field of serious historical drama, a region the French regarded almost as a private preserve. After considerable anticipation, the play proved a triple disappointment. Although Mr. Wallack had called in a French actress, Mme Saint Léon, to play the role of Volumnia in English, the interpretation of the play was considered quite unsatisfactory. The *Globe* of August 8 commented sternly:

What illusion can be created by a primping tribune, a sulky Menius, a Volumnia showing neither pride nor maternal tenderness? We were denied even the satisfaction of seeing a true Coriolanus in Mr. Wallack. He shouts the role from beginning to end without the slightest variation.

Wallack's unfortunate bellowing had killed the main role and none of the other actors retrieved the play in any way. The critic of *La Pandore* termed the evening "a colourless and at times almost ridiculous presentation." Of the leading actor the same critic judiciously remarked:

Wallack as Coriolanus gave the same impression as in Rollo or Othello. He has good presence, his speech is resonant and pleasing to the ear, he even tries to be tragic; but in moments of passion, his gestures, countenance, his whole interpretation take on a forced and exaggerated quality which exceeds truth.

No doubt there was similar justice in the reference to Mme Saint Léon:

Her costume and bearing indicate good taste and a certain grace which we French do not always attribute to English actresses. As for her interpretation in Volumnia twas no worse than that of our most experienced actresses.

It is interesting that the critics remarked stringently on inaccuracy and anachronism in the staging, although here facilities may have been lacking. All the critics fiercely and very justifiably condemned the massacre of Shakespeare's play by its arrangers and adapters. Not satisfied with slashing the original, they had inflicted upon it several sections of James Thomson's pithless version of the same subject. Perhaps this juxtaposition lent added splendour, by contrast, to the authentic Shakespeare, but this was nevertheless a dubious result.

On the first of August, Wallack attempted an unfortunate double bill: *The Stranger* and *The Merchant of Venice*. The former adapted from Kotzebue, had been given several times the year before and therefore brought nothing new. The latter, so difficult for the French to grasp, had been accepted only because of Kean's superb portrayal of Shylock; Wallack was no Kean.

One week later came the drama *Douglas*, Mr. Wallack's benefit performance. The evening was marked principally by a skirmish during the intermission between the supporters and detractors of Mrs. West, who was again taking a role. The brawl, as gleefully reported by the *Courrier des théâtres*, began in the *parterre* but spilled out into the corridors and even into the foyer. Only after the police had ejected a number of the most obstreperous combatants was sufficient order established to proceed with the play.

For the closing performance on August 11, the company offered *Jane Shore*. This play had gained its popularity in 1827–8 chiefly because of Harriet Smithson's exceptional acting. Since Mrs. West had failed to please the public, Wallack again called on Mme Saint Léon to carry the title role. For once the *Courrier* approved of something about the visitors—the presence of a French actress playing a tragic role with dignity and good taste. The compliment included a thrust at Miss Smithson, principal target of the *Courrier*, as the primary female figure of the first English company: Mme Saint Léon's "good taste prevented her from indulging, during the last act, in the contortions to which we saw an English actress abandon herself, amazed as she was at Parisian applause." After the first three performances the more moderate critics, realizing that the troupe had nothing very new or significant to offer, ceased to refer to them.

Wallack and his cast must be given credit for a strenuous effort to please the public. With modest means, both personal and material, they had presented a wide range of plays and had persisted after disappointments. Although they were not greeted with the animosity of 1822, they most certainly did not rouse the response of 1828. "We believe that the English troupe has had enough. We too," was the *Courrier's* surly announcement of the end of their visit. The more gracious *Pandore* commented on Wallack's benefit performance: "It would be well if the Paris public roused itself, this once at least, from the indifference which it has displayed toward the presence of the English actors in Paris."

By the following year only one of the English players—Harriet Smithson—was to be found in the capital. Either because of her indifferent welcome in England or because of some affection for the city that had afforded her such triumphs, Miss Smithson again tried her fortunes in Paris. In March, 1830, she took a role with the Opéra Comique company in their pantomime production, *L'Auberge d'Auray*. As she could not speak French, Miss Smithson had a completely mute part. None the less, she won enthusiastic receptions for her acting from both public and critics, although the play was inferior. By a cruel stroke of fate, the theatre to which she had given such good service went bankrupt shortly afterward, with its actors unpaid. A long and pitiable letter from the distressed young woman to the King himself remained in an official pigeon-hole.[2] Finally, on December 5 her fellow artists came to her rescue with a benefit evening at the Opéra which raised nine thousand francs for her. Miss Smithson appeared in the production (Auber's *Masaniello*), playing the role of the dumb girl, Fenella.

[2] J. L. Borgerhoff in *Le Théâtre anglais à Paris sous la Restauration* (Paris, 1912) reproduces this letter in an appendix.

Some eighteen months later, in the autumn of 1832, this courageous if foolishly persistent woman attempted to establish a troupe of her own in Paris. Although she was unable to recruit a completely satisfactory company, it was nevertheless reasonably capable, with Mr. Archer as leading man. Miss Smithson had obtained the right to give performances on alternate nights at the Théâtre Italien and the Odéon. On November 21 she opened at the Odéon with *Jane Shore*. Unfortunately the company was not well supported; on December 5 Southerne's *Isabella or the Fatal Marriage* failed utterly. After attempting a few more popular favourites, and even *Hamlet* on December 31, the company abandoned the regular theatres and took refuge in the little Chantereine hall where Mr. Penley had given his plays in 1822. On January 17 the critic of the *Revue et gazette des théâtres* wrote: "For my part, I am sorry that the English players should have abandoned a theatre where the public, quitting its initial indifference, would probably have gone to patronize them."

In the somewhat pretentious London *Court Journal*, January, 1833, passing references to the determined directress appear in the items from the Paris correspondent. Under date of January 26 he reported:

Miss Smithson's company is still performing in the Rue Chantereine and the fair actress displays her histrionic skill as admirably as ever. The principal actor is Mr. Archer who *certes* is an equal match with most of the French tragic actors of the hour. Macready was, or maybe is, expected, but it is said that he demands £35 sterling per performance! *Par exemple*, Monsieur Macready, whence is the cash to come? The little theatre is well attended *sans doute*, but at that rate the great favourite like Aaron's rod would swallow up all the receipts. N.B. This is not official though I believe it to be true. The plays are well selected chiefly from Shakespeare.

The careless tone of this passage suggests that the writer did not know the true situation. He was less optimistic a week later when he commented briefly, "The English theatrical company in Paris are going on very indifferently."

The performances aroused very little comment in the Paris journals and since Berlioz, who does refer to them, is typically inaccurate in his dates and heroically refrained from attending the plays despite his attachment to Miss Smithson, virtually no details about them remain. Berlioz does, however, report that the unfortunate directress was becoming involved in complete financial ruin when she broke a leg and was forced to abandon her venture completely. At the time of her accident Miss Smithson had been organizing a benefit performance for herself and Berlioz threw himself into the final organization of this. The performance, which took place on April 2, raised a sum sufficient to clear the most pressing of her debts.[3]

The valiant attempts Berlioz made to explain the collapse are rather touching. The novelty of Shakespeare, he suggests, had already palled on the fickle public since the Romantics had won the battle for the stage. He even hints darkly that apprehensive authors may have plotted against the English players, fearing that such productions would reveal their own borrowings from Shakespeare.

At this point Berlioz comes so prominently to the centre of the stage that his relationship with Miss Smithson must be briefly reviewed.[4] At the first performance of *Hamlet* in September, 1827, young Berlioz had been smitten by the impact both of Shakespeare and of the lovely actress; his letters of the following months contain constant references to these wonderful beings. At first he remained unknown to the actress, but, toward the end of 1828, declared himself; in February, 1829, he reported a sign of encouragement. But in March, refusing to see her admirer, Miss Smithson departed for Holland and England. After a full year Berlioz once more met his idol, but their relationship ended after a tempestuous interview. His Italian sojourn followed, during which he became engaged to Camille Moke. The brusque cancellation of the engagement by the girl's mother drove Berlioz to an attempt at suicide. Unable to bear his exile, the musician returned before his scholarship expired, and arrived in Paris just before the English productions of 1832 were presented. To reintroduce himself to Miss Smithson, Berlioz prepared a concert of his own works inspired by her, and arranged to have her attend without her knowing the programme. A dramatic reunion took place at the concert itself. Even the reconciliation, however, did not halt Miss Smithson's last efforts to carry on her presentations. The young musician's generosity in completing arrangements for Miss Smithson's benefit performance brought the two artists more closely together. Yet by August Berlioz was again quarreling fiercely with her. At one point he took poison in her presence, and, when he recovered, he threatened to go to Ger-

[3] Hector Berlioz, *Mémoires* (Paris, 1870), *passim* 1831-3.
[4] The events of these years (1827-36) may be traced in the *Mémoires* and the *Lettres intimes* of Berlioz although his dates must be checked carefully in contemporary sources.

many. In desperation, Miss Smithson consented to their marriage, which took place on October 3 of that year. At a further concert organized by Berlioz, his wife appeared as Ophelia in the fourth act of *Hamlet*, the supporting roles being carried by a number of English amateurs. Though still somewhat uncertain of herself after her accident, she was "heart rending, sublime, and applauded to the echo," her husband reports; elsewhere he attributes Mme Dorval's even more tumultuous reception to a well-paid claque.

Mme Berlioz did not cease to long for the footlights. Part of her desire to act arose from her laudable anxiety to help her struggling husband. Berlioz reports, late in 1833, his wife's regretful refusal of a place in Charles Kemble's company on the ground that she was insufficiently recovered from her accident to carry full roles. There is something peculiar about this reputed offer. If it was made it would have been both typical and worthy of Kemble; there had been sneering suggestions in England that the "accident" had been merely a means of escape from difficulties although there is no doubt that her recuperation was painfully slow. In any case Mme Berlioz remained in France, a vague offer to play English tragedy in Prussia having come to nothing. Early in 1834 she dallied with the idea of recruiting an amateur English troupe to present plays in public but lack of available personnel halted this project.

In October and November of 1834 the opportunity of a mimed role came in the pantomime play *La Dernière Heure d'un condamné* at the Théâtre Nautique. In spite of her excellent performance, she was again cheated of her wages by the failure of the theatre. Engrossed in the care of her little son and handicapped by her lack of French, Mme Berlioz did not appear on the stage again until December, 1836, when, in a special performance given at the Théâtre des Variétés, she won a kindly notice from Jules Janin. The following year brings the last mention of a public appearance by this once idolized figure. In May she appeared with something of her old brilliance as Jane Shore, this reading taking place at a special *soirée* given at the home of M. de Castellane. Finally, at the special summer *Fêtes de Versailles* organized in July of the same year, she carried a *rôle de figurante*, receiving afterward the thanks of the Duchesse d'Orléans and a handsome gift.

Berlioz deplored the termination of his wife's momentarily brilliant career. For years after their marriage he importuned his dramatist friends to write plays including a pantomime role. But even Hugo could not oblige, and the composer's pleas to George Sand after the appearance of *Mauprat* were also without avail. The two even considered going to America, where her lack of French would be no handicap and he might escape his enemies, but hesitated because of their small child. At his wife's death, the composer accused himself (an extremely rare procedure with him) of having blocked her career, although he may have been indulging in one of his frequent extravagant outbursts.

The last years of Miss Smithson's life were profoundly sad. Separated from her volcanic husband, lonely in a foreign land, paralysed and mute, this woman, who had really introduced Shakespeare to Paris, died in 1854 after nearly two decades of obscurity.

We may dismiss the egocentric fatuities which Hugo and Liszt addressed to her husband at her death, but perhaps the lyric and sincere tribute of her friend Janin may be taken as her literary epitaph:

In her pure, sonorous, golden voice, there rang forth in triumphant, immortal tones the prose and poetry of Shakespeare. She won the sympathy and admiration of her hearers . . . . She led the way for Mme Dorval, Frédéric Lemaitre, Mme Malibran, Victor Hugo, Berlioz! She was called Juliette; she was called Ophelia.[5]

Or we may listen to Rachel as, standing with Janin before the portrait of the actress whom as a small child she had seen in Paris, she freely admitted her debt to the sweet Irish player.

[5]Jules Janin, *Almanach de la littérature du théâtre et des beaux arts* (Paris, 1853–69; 3 vols.), I, *Almanach pour l'année 1854*.

10 · "Well Have We Done, Thrice Valiant Countrymen"

When bidding the English players farewell in 1828, M. Saint Eloy of *L'Incorruptible*, wrote of Macready: "He is leaving; let us hope that a few months hence we will be able to see and admire him again." This wish was not to be fulfilled: some seventeen years were to elapse before that distinguished actor again appeared in Paris. Long absence did not indicate either pique or forgetfulness on his part, for Macready had reason to remember his Paris experiences with special satisfaction. He had been greeted from the first with approval, his reputation had risen steadily, comparisons between Kean and himself had all been in his favour, and both his visits had been financially rewarding.

His continued interest in France is revealed in many ways. In 1838, while managing Covent Garden, he received M. Dumanoir, director of the Variétés, who was seeking to bring a French troupe to London; unfortunately, conditions at the time did not permit Macready to accept the offer. In July, 1838, when he visited Paris, he saw Mme Dorval at the Théâtre du Gymnase and greatly admired her portrayal of a jealous, frustrated woman in *La Belle-Sœur*. A few months later, in March, 1839, the play *Richelieu*, which he produced from Bulwer-Lytton's version, brought him into repeated and delightful contact with Alfred de Vigny, then on a visit to London. Having received various suggestions from the author of *Cinq Mars*, which had made Vigny for months the "intimate enemy" of Richelieu, Macready eagerly awaited the French poet's verdict on the play. Vigny greatly admired the performances, and the actor reports further lengthy profitable and pleasant conversations with him.

The next year Dumas, after seeing Macready in *Hamlet*, told him that he was intending to translate the play for presentation in Paris. Apparently the thought of visiting France again in a professional capacity was in the actor's mind, for, after Dumas' visit, he spoke on different occasions with his leading lady, Helena Faucit, regarding a Paris visit. Thoughts of France were also kept fresh in his mind by continued correspondence with a French friend and admirer, Marcellin de Fresne, a well-known figure in Parisian official and literary circles. The London visit of Rachel, who as a child, had seen Macready in 1828, gave an additional impetus to the desire to return to France. Macready was disappointed in Rachel's performance in *Cinna*, but in *Horace* she convinced him of her greatness.

At the close of the 1842-3 Drury Lane season, the exorbitant demands of the proprietors obliged Macready to disband his company. The following year he carried out a lengthy American tour, while Miss Faucit filled various successful engagements in Britain. In the autumn of 1844 Mr. Mitchell, the energetic promoter of the French theatre in Bond Street, approached Miss Faucit with the proposal that she should present a group of English plays in Paris, and that on his return from America, Macready should join her. These presentations were to alternate with those of the Théâtre Italien, and Mr. Mitchell guaranteed that if the plays did not prove successful the engagement would be completed in his Bond Street theatre in London.

Mr. Mitchell had assembled a strong company. Macready, still known and admired from his visits of 1828, returned with greater maturity and experience. In Bennett and Chapman, he had two reliable lieutenants; Mrs. Mathurin, the second lady, had for years carried her roles successfully in London; and finally, the young Helena Faucit proved to be a powerful attraction to audiences and critics alike. Although only twenty-seven, Miss Faucit had had nearly ten years of acting experience, largely with such actors as Kemble and Macready. She too had already visited France, going to Paris in 1841 with her brother on a recuperative holiday journey. A letter from Macready to M. de Fresne had introduced her to that gentleman and they quickly became friends. Under her host's guidance, she had not only frequented the best Saint-Germain society but had also met Chateaubriand, Delaroche, and other celebrities. At the theatre she had admired Mlle Mars' beauty of voice and bearing without being greatly impressed by her acting. The performances of Rachel, on the contrary, she found deeply impressive, and the two young actresses greatly enjoyed their social contacts. In 1844, quite aside from the splendid artistry which made her for decades the leading interpreter of the chief Shakespearian heroines, Miss Faucit already possessed what the French critics quickly appreciated: a personal character of such strength and beauty as to elevate any role she played. Though the general supporting cast contained no outstanding names, it impressed the Paris critics favourably throughout the series of plays.

Miss Faucit preceded Macready to France, but he arrived early in December with the intention of opening on the fourth. A severe fall, in which he narrowly escaped breaking a leg, necessitated two postponements to await his full recovery. Finally, on December 16, the company opened with *Othello*, the same play in which Penley had faced the rabid crowds of 1822. Under that date Macready wrote in his journal:

Acted *Othello* with great care, often with much reality; but I could not feel the sympathy of the audience; they were fashionable, and from the construction of the theatre not within reach of my electric contact, to coin a phrase; the shocking delay between the acts was another cause for a certain heaviness which I felt to pervade the evening. I was not satisfied with the issue, uneasy and restless in mind.[1]

The diaries of this sensitive Irishman abound in such troubled judgments, belied by enthusiastic curtain calls and flattering press reports. But on this critical night even the approval of Charles Dickens, the warm congratulations of Dumas and of the leading French actor Régnier, left him unhappy.

The press reports, though varied, were a considerable reassurance. *La France théâtrale* commented: "The actors whom Mr. Mitchell has just brought from London opened in the Théâtre Italien. Shakespeare's *Othello* was played to the satisfaction of a large audience." Its references to the interpreters were equally brief. "The honours of the evening went to Macready. Miss Helen Faucit has qualities, but where is the grace of our French actresses?" The incurably Anglophobe *Courrier des spectacles*, dealing with the chief role, declared: "Macready seemed inevitably destined to dominate. His delivery does not lack force and warmth. But he does not escape the monotony of that style." And sacrificing gallantry to patriotic zeal it continued: "Mme Faucit has qualities which are more esteemed in her own country than among us, where we seek more naturalness and a more communicative sensitivity."

On the other hand, the *Journal des débats* in a combined criticism of

---

[1] *Diaries of Wm. C. Macready*, ed. W. Toynbee (London, 1912). All other quotations from Macready's journals are taken from this work.

Hamlet which was given on the eighteenth, and *Othello*, which was repeated on the twentieth, gave unreserved praise to all concerned. In a lengthy study of Hamlet's character, the writer suggested that the Prince of Denmark could never have been properly appreciated by Shakespeare's contemporaries. The melancholy Dane, in his anguished debate, he saw as a colossal Romantic figure and this mighty conception of Shakespeare had appeared before them: "The true Shakespeare, the great William, appeared once more on the French stage with an interpreter worthy of him." These remarks on *Hamlet* must have been especially welcome to Macready, whose Hamlet had been considered the weakest of his roles in 1828. Now the critic showed unlimited enthusiasm. "While doing justice to the superlative qualities which Macready displayed in *Othello* . . . we find him incomparably superior in the role of Hamlet." After the usual comments on the demanding nature of the part we read: "But Macready's talent so intelligent, so literary, so deeply meditative, makes him splendidly fitted to interpret Hamlet." This high praise did not amaze those who knew Macready's literary background and richly sensitive, thoughtful nature.

Dumas, contrasting the various interpretations of Othello which he had seen, describes Macready's version: "With Macready he was an Arab of the time of the Abencérages, lofty and chivalrous." In spite of the frequent condemnations of English actors for their melodramatic death scenes, Dumas approved Macready's version of Othello's death. Having described the varied fashions in which the actors whom he had seen in the role delivered the suicidal stab, he reported the Irish actor's distinctive performance: "Then Macready added a most effective touch: once stricken, he still rallied the strength to move to the bed and gasping Desdemona's name, he sank down to die, with his lips on the hand of his victim."[2]

Miss Faucit had to withstand a double comparison from the more mature members of her audiences. She was compared with first, the brilliant artist opposite whom she was playing, and secondly, the memories of those for whom Harriet Smithson's Ophelia still remained the ultimate in poignant wistfulness. Nevertheless, her Desdemona received kindly criticism from the *Journal des débats*. Appreciation came also from the *Messager* where Edouard Thierry, a delicate and discriminating critic, wrote: "Hence before the end of the evening

[2] A. Dumas, *Souvenirs dramatiques* (Paris, 1868; 2 vols.), II, p. 123.

the public was already dividing its attention between Othello and Desdemona. It knew that London had sent it not only a great tragedian but a great tragic actress." Equally gratifying praise rewarded her interpretation of Ophelia: "Ophelia could not be imagined more touching or more graceful." And the familiar comment on the English genius for dramatic action appears: "Our French audience remained amazed at her pantomime, so full of good sense, of ideas, of tenderness, of passion but in particular full of restraint and modesty." The last two of these qualities, by their classic nature, seem to suggest a reason for the French critic's warmth of approval. Even Macready, the sternest of critics, declared her handling of the mad scenes excellent. Writing to Sir Theodore Martin over thirty years later, Régnier remarked: "I have never since read or seen *Othello* or *Hamlet* without recalling Lady Martin as Desdemona and Ophelia, and I still retain in my mind as one of my most striking dramatic memories the evening when she played the role of Lady Macbeth for the first time in Paris."[3]

On December 23 the company presented *Virginius*, a play in which Macready had made a powerful impression in 1828. His own comment, "Acted *Virginius* with much energy and power to a very excited audience," suggests the success of the presentation. Indeed, the audience clamoured for his appearance at the end of the fourth act. But he felt it unbecoming to the dignity of his art to appear, and waited until the end of the play when the calls developed into an ovation. Miss Faucit's Virginia called forth special appreciation; the spoken role totals barely sixty lines scattered over four acts but Miss Faucit, none the less, caught and reflected the spirit of the heroine and her portrayal of the role greatly impressed the critics. Four days later the play was repeated before an audience which Macready described as deeply interested but not so tumultuous in their applause. But as on the first presentation, a gratifying call for curtain appearances concluded the evening. Mention of audience interest recalls Miss Faucit's reactions. Writing years later, she remembered in particular the special atmosphere of these performances:

I could not help feeling that I drew my audience with me. And what an audience it was! No obtrusive applause, for there was no organized claque for the English plays, but what an indescribable air of sympathy surrounded me. Every tone was heard, every look was watched, felt, appreciated.[4]

---
[3]Sir Theodore Martin, *Helena Faucit, Lady Martin* (London, 1900), p. 124. Miss Faucit married Mr. Theodore (afterwards Sir Theodore) Martin in 1851.
[4]*Ibid.*, p. 68.

Hamlet, which made such a favourable impression throughout the season, was billed again for the thirtieth, and passed off without any remarkable feature except that Miss Faucit, not being able to appear, was replaced by Mrs. Serle.

On January 1 Macready wrote: "Acted *Werner* with great care and power to a bad and unsympathetic audience. I would not give in. I think I acted well, was called for." This play, written by Lord Byron, had been consistently performed during Macready's American tour, and he seems to have had a considerable liking for it. There is no doubt that he acted the role well. Thomas Marshall speaks in the most flattering terms of Macready's handling of Werner.

> In this lifeless and shadowy part of an insipid and heavy tragedy, Macready's masterly display of power and pathos, investing an imperfect outline of the victim of an overweening pride, with vitality and forcible expression, rose almost to sublimity.[5]

And in his *Leaves from an Actor's Note-Book*, George Vandenhoff, no lover of Macready (whom he regarded as a martinet) describes Werner as "a character which Macready played to perfection leaving nothing to be desired."

Apparently, however, the play created an unfavourable impression on the Paris audience, since it was not repeated. An examination of the special text published for the presentations suggests that this sombre historical tragedy, written in 1823, resembled rather too closely the Gothic productions of Dumas and Hugo. In 1844 the French public had suffered a distinct surfeit of these as the poor reception of *Les Burgraves* some months previously had demonstrated. The fact that Miss Faucit did not appear in the cast may also have affected the success of the play.

After another performance of *Hamlet* three days later, the troupe launched a series of three consecutive performances of *Macbeth*. This play had not only proved consistently acceptable to French audiences in 1828, but had also provided a thoroughly successful role for Macready. The actor's own comments on the opening performance January 6 are particularly interesting. "Acted Macbeth, in my opinion, better than I have ever done before. The audience was deeply attentive and interested, but did not give the quantity of applause which such a performance would have elicited in England." A number of possible answers suggest themselves. Macready's own judgment did not always

[5] Thos. Marshall, *Lives of the Most Celebrated Actors and Actresses* (London, 1848), p. 17.

coincide with that of his audience, though it must be granted that he usually erred in the direction of pessimism. What to him were ultimate touches of excellence may, in the setting and hall, have eluded the bulk of his audience, and they may also have been in intonations or gestures unfamiliar to a Gallic audience. The whole matter of the way in which the English handled the supernatural on the stage must also be taken into account. On the whole the French were not greatly pleased or impressed by the English rendition of such scenes. The ghost of Hamlet's father, so controversial among English producers, caused endless dispute in French circles; the witches in *Macbeth* aroused laughter or disgusted condemnation according to the delicacy of the onlookers; and the spectral appearances of the banquet scene caused much discussion between those demanding a physical presence and those favouring an empty chair. Taking all these problems into consideration, it may seem surprising that Macready regularly won such good receptions in these plays.

On the following Wednesday Macready again played Macbeth and recorded: "Not so well as Monday, but I think with power and discrimination." Then follows a wry tribute to his leading lady: "The audience applauded Miss Faucit's sleeping scene much more than anything else in the whole play." The audience had sound reason for approving the actress's performance. After remarking upon the extreme variance between the elegiac passivity of Virginia and the fierce energy of Lady Macbeth, and emphasizing the difficulty of interpreting them both adequately, M. Thierry continued, "They are two such dissimilar natures that one human being could scarcely seem able to represent them both, but a grasp of fundamentals lifts an artist above the physical, and in the sleepwalking scene Miss Faucit rose to the most gripping depiction of terror."

On the tenth, for Miss Faucit's benefit performance, *Macbeth* again gave the popular actress an opportunity to prove her capacities to an especially large audience. And, also selecting a role in which he had gained special favour, Macready chose *Hamlet* for his benefit performance on the thirteenth, acting the Prince as he tells us "for the most part extremely well, the audience were interested and attentive but not so excitable as usual." Parody being almost a tribute in France, it seems significant that the *Journal des théâtres* of January 8 reported enthusiastically on the clever mimicry of André Hoffman, a parodist at the Théâtre des Variétés, in a vaudeville entitled "English Importation." Particularly admired was his imitation of Macready in the role of Othello: "Costume, bearing, diction, all were authentically rendered by the artist."

Although the series had now been concluded, three highly interesting evenings remained. On Thursday, the sixteenth of January, the company appeared at the handsomely appointed theatre of the Tuileries palace for a command performance before Louis Philippe, the Queen, and an impressive array of personalities. For this occasion Macready prepared an abridged version of *Hamlet*, the most notable excision being the grave-diggers' scene. Knowing that the response both in comprehension and in applause would be extremely limited, he resolved to devote himself exclusively to the interpretation of his role. The play went well, although court etiquette kept the applause within decorous limits. It is amusing to read of Victor Hugo holding himself in check with difficulty, as his enthusiasm threatened to carry him beyond these bounds. After the performance, both the leading actors received individual tokens of the king's pleasure. As an after-piece, the junior members of the company presented *The Day after the Wedding*, in which Robert Wyndham particularly distinguished himself as Colonel Freelove.

The following night the troupe offered a special double bill—the fourth act of *Henry IV* and three acts of *Romeo and Juliet*. This particular presentation was Mr. Mitchell's benefit performance as promoter of the visit. Aware of Miss Faucit's disappointment at not having played the role of Juliet, Mitchell chose the portions of that play in which her powers would be most tellingly displayed. The death scene from *Henry IV*, on the other hand, gave full scope for Macready's capacities. These two selections also satisfied a French call for further presentation of the Shakespeare historical plays, and for a taste of tragic romance. Once again Miss Faucit carried off special honours as Juliet; in this role she attained the pinnacle of her success in Paris. Admiring the ability of the actress to submerge herself in the character, the critic of *Le Messager* wrote: "It is one of the marks of Miss Faucit's talent that her countenance explains everything ... it is an open book, a magic book if you will, where each reads in his own language." Turning to her voice, he rose to even higher praise: "I appeal to the memories of those who attended *Romeo and Juliet*, the memories of those who do not know English. Was there a single word of . . . that charming confession of Juliet which was not understood as if it had been spoken in a universal language as it fell from Miss Helen's lips?"

The last appearance was on the eighteenth, when the selection from *Henry IV* formed part of an evening organized at the Opéra Comique on behalf of the Commission de la Société des auteurs dramatiques français, the benevolent society for distressed authors. This was Macready's sole performance before the general public. At the beginning of the presentation, one individual attempted to interrupt by mimicking the actor's voice but was instantly suppressed; after this the play received deep attention. The evening concluded agreeably in Macready's dressing-room, where the Committee waited upon their guest with an address of appreciation signed by Scribe, Hugo, Halévy, and others and a handsome gold medal struck for the occasion.

Macready's more relaxed moments in Paris were also of considerable value. The journey was in one sense a reunion with a number of personal friends. Before performing at all he was welcomed by his admiring correspondent, M. de Fresne, who constituted himself an almost embarrassingly solicitous host. During the wait before the opening day, the distinguished actor met the leading figure at the Comédie Française, M. Régnier. On December 11 he attended the Théâtre Français, seeing Mlle George play in Dumas' *Christine*. "So dull a play," he wrote, "I scarcely ever saw."

On December 28 de Fresne entertained for Macready, the guests including Delaroche the painter, Régnier, Bertin the powerful editor of the *Journal des débats*, and a son of the actor Talma. Macready's French was quite adequate in a cultured company, and he thoroughly enjoyed the gathering. The following afternoon he visited Vigny and his invalid English wife. The evening after the first presentation of *Hamlet* in 1845, he had dinner with Sue and accompanied the dramatist to the Comédie Française, where they saw *Guerrero*, a melodramatic Mexican play. His comments on the chief actors show how active his critical faculties were: "Mlle Plessis was sometimes graceful, but not quite concentrated enough in her passion. M. Beauvalet was melodramatic in his style, strong, but sometimes beyond the modesty of nature." The following day the indefatigable de Fresne carried his guest off to the Ecole des Beaux Arts to visit Delaroche. The school, which Macready describes as "a building and institution to shame the

British people," obviously made a deep impression upon him. Later in the day he was introduced to an elderly gentleman who had actually known the eighteenth century giants of the stage Garrick and Lekain; although much interested, Macready seems to have been somewhat saddened by the recollections of these actors' lives, and hints that he scarcely envied them.

That same day his manager Mr. Mitchell informed him that, as the result of a government ruling, their visit would have to be concluded immediately. No reasons were given, but the difficulty must have been overcome since the visit continued for ten days more, and thus extended even beyond the period planned. In her reminiscences Miss Faucit refers to malicious rumour, according to which the prohibition had come in response to pressure from French actors. This groundless slur on a group which had given assiduous attendance to the English players and heartily accepted their English colleagues, happily had no effect on their further relations.

Free from theatrical responsibilities after the eighteenth of January, Macready remained in the capital to enjoy a few more days of social pleasures. The following morning he called on a M. Leduc, who "told me of the enthusiasm of the literary men in Paris on my acting." From this gentleman's home he proceeded to the Place Royale to call on Victor Hugo. The house he found "quite a poet's mansion," and Hugo himself he described as "most earnest in his expressions of admiration and respect for me."

The following day, January 20, he visited George Sand, with whom he had a long conversation on Shakespeare and on England, and whom he "liked . . . very much." At this time Mme Sand was just beginning to be interested in the stage, for which she wrote a number of items, chiefly adaptations from her own novels but also translations from Shakespeare. That evening Macready encountered another translator in the person of Barbier, who was then translating *Julius Caesar* into French prose.

Towards the end of his sojourn in Paris, the great actor's compatriots finally awoke to his presence. On the twelfth of January he enjoyed a pleasant evening with an assorted English company. On the twentieth, he attended a brilliant reception at the British ambassador's, where the guests watched an amateur production of several scenes from *The School for Scandal* and a farce, *The Merry Monarch*. The actor's comment,

"To me it was all amusing," should not perhaps be taken as too supercilious for he carries on with favourable remarks on several performers, although he does comment with some acerbity on the airy fashion in which amateurs undertake dramatic productions.

On his last day in the capital, he reluctantly accompanied his friend de Fresne to the Conservatoire of the state theatres. His comment is revealing:

Heard the pupils of Samson go through their course of theatrical instruction. It is an institution of the government to train pupils, who are elected to the school, for the stage. I was interested, and saw the inefficacy of the system clearly; it was teaching *conventionalism*—it was perpetuating the mannerisms of the French stage which is all mannerism. Genius would be cramped if not maimed and distorted by such a course.

During his visit Macready, like Garrick before him in 1765, considered the possibility of appearing on the French stage. The thought was that he should take the role of Oreste in the original French of Racine's *Andromaque*, with Rachel playing opposite him. But after considering the difficulties, he followed his predecessor's example and gave up the idea.

Miss Faucit was meanwhile enjoying a pronounced social success, especially in the salon of Mme Ancelot, where her youth and ingenuous charm surprised and delighted those who met her. Her acting left lasting memories among those who saw her in 1844. Dumas, who attended her performances faithfully in spite of his total ignorance of English, expressed his determination to write a play for her based on the French career of the Princess Henriette d'Angleterre.

Macready returned to London after a series of very successful presentations which left keen satisfaction. The opinion in cultured circles is well suggested by a few lines from the address accompanying the gold medal from the French *Auteurs Dramatiques* as quoted in Macready's *Reminiscences* under January 18: "The support which you have just lent us could not increase the admiration that Paris holds for your talent; but it has enhanced the esteem that we hold for your noble and generous character."[6]

The results of this visit were of course in no way comparable to those of the 1827-8 seasons. The struggle of classic and romantic for the French stage which was raging so hotly in 1828 had long since been won. In fact, as the reception of *Werner* suggests, it had been won

[6]Wm. Macready, *Reminiscences*, ed. Sir F. Pollock (London, 1876).

and lost again. The fact is that Hugo and Dumas did not create a great school or tradition in the French theatre. Indeed, William Archer in his volume of essays, *About the Theatre*, suggests that if Hugo's dramatic works had not existed there would really not be any notable break in the development of French drama; we would simply lose a number of very enjoyable plays. In 1844 the public were much more accustomed to the Shakespearean type of drama. As the music critic of the *Journal des débats* (none other than Hector Berlioz) remarked in the issue of December 29:

> Macready and the tragedies of Shakespeare attract three times a week ... that intelligent and enthusiastic public which Victor Hugo, Alexandre Dumas, and Alfred de Vigny so laboriously formed. Oh, that I were a literary man so that I might have the right to discuss the great actor and the wonders of Shakespeare.

Berlioz' article actually concerned a notable work being rehearsed at that moment in Paris, Dr. Locke's chorus from *Macbeth* in English with a specially engaged English vocalist to sing the role of Hecate. The mild renaissance of classical drama which took place at the time of Macready's visit and centred around Ponsard as author and Rachel as interpreter, was not calculated to cause rioting in or outside any theatre.

With the exception of a few intransigents, led by Charles Maurice of the *Courrier des spectacles*, the critics were almost embarrassingly generous in their praises. As for the actors, Macready's French colleagues supported their display of social amenities by the sincerest form of flattery, imitation. In its issue of December 22 the *Courrier des spectacles* grudgingly remarked on the visitors' acting: "As for their style of acting, those of our artists who call themselves the modern school have imitated them so closely, that these foreigners cannot show us anything in that line which will surprise us." Indeed, Macready's comment on the hero of *Guerrero* would lead us to believe that the French artists were perhaps outdoing their models.

We might say of the visit that, since no great battle was fought, no resounding victory was won but that it was certainly not without influence. "Beyond doubt," writes a contemporary critic, "the visit of the English actors in 1844-1845 gave a powerful impulse to 'the Shakespearean movement,' and it may have been the cause of dissolution for the 'common sense' tragedy which must have compared unfavourably with the more forcible, more vivid and at the same time, more philosophical dramas of the great English playwright."[7] Financially the venture must have proved satisfactory, since Mr. Mitchell made strenuous efforts to arrange a second tour with Miss Faucit as leading lady.

Neither of the chief performers acted again in Paris. Miss Faucit, however, spent a short time there in the spring of 1859 and although she made no public appearance, her visit constituted a genuine triumph. At the home of M. de Fresne, the unsuspecting artist was brought to a large salon where upwards of two hundred chosen friends awaited her. With only a brief pause, the guest of honour gave a brilliant interpretation of scenes from *Macbeth* and from *Romeo and Juliet*, with her host reading opposite her. This *soirée*, to Miss Faucit's surprise, caused a considerable stir in the capital. Writing in *L'Union*, M. Henry de Riancey enthusiastically reported of the great actress: "By a contrast which is rare indeed, she is as passionate and as pensive in the role of Juliet as she is sombre and gloomy in that of Lady Macbeth." And, summing up the performance, he commented: "The talent of the skilful artist impressed and delighted us all."

Macready paid a brief visit to Paris in 1856. He enjoyed hearing the prima donna Ristori, then high in favour, and visited his friends Régnier and George Sand. The latter's adaptation of *As You Like It* was then being given on the stage; Macready's critical integrity forced him to describe it as a failure despite excellent interpretation. Though he never again appeared on a Paris stage, he cherished kindly feelings towards France until his death. Among those who acted in the French capital, he probably did as much as even Miss Smithson to make the great plays of English literature more comprehensible and more popular. And Miss Faucit, Mademoiselle Hélène, remained a fragrant memory in Parisian minds for many years.

[7] Eric Partridge, *The French Romantics' Knowledge of English Literature (1820–1848)* (Paris, 1924), pp. 206–7.

11 · History Repeats Itself

After Mr. Macready's happy experiences of 1844-5, ten years elapsed before another British theatrical troupe appeared in Paris. In June, 1855, the *Revue des théâtres* briefly announced that an English company under the management of M. Alphonse Ruin de Fye would open at the Théâtre Italien. The visitors were to alternate with a visiting Italian opera troupe led by Mme Ristori.

The manager and leading actor, William Wallack, was a nephew of the Wallack whose visit had come, anticlimactically, after the important season of 1828. The younger actor showed to modest advantage in serious drama, where he utilized a robust physique and a voice which possessed both power and variety. His wife, a tragedienne of considerable talent, frequently played opposite him and the chief secondary roles were taken by Miss Cleveland and George Bennett. As the chief item for their debut the company selected *Macbeth*.

In his brief critique of the opening on June 15, M. Retz felt that he was not sufficiently familiar with the actors to judge them adequately and limited himself to noting the success of the chief interpreters who had "shown excellent talent in their roles." A one-act sketch by Coyne entitled *Un Pas de Fascination* had been well received, and an additional presentation of a ballet pantomime was much applauded. The promotors had provided a large company and its members did not fail in quality. The correspondent for *Le Théâtre*, Ernest Dubreuil, waxed very enthusiastic over the staging on the opening evening. "The settings," he declared, "are complete and well designed, and strange as it may seem the extras are all pretty." He especially admired Miss Simpson in the part of Hecate and even suggested that Parisian managers might well bring over a few *figurantes* from London.

In his later discussion of *Macbeth*, the same critic reported on June 20: "Although few of the audience understood the language, *Macbeth* was carefully listened to. Shakespeare's genius swept one along; what the ear failed to grasp the mind could guess." His reactions to the interpretation were also favourable. "Mr. Wallack," he wrote, "played Macbeth with great skill and was warmly applauded, especially in the banquet scene." In his later, more comprehensive critique M. Retz of the *Revue* began by suggesting that the utterly unfamiliar English method of playing Shakespeare might well cause some astonishment: "Mr. and Mrs. Wallack display a violence which at first looks like exaggeration to us, but which is simply a necessity in view of the literature which they are interpreting." To sustain the loftiness of Shakespearean moods, he felt, demanded unremitting exertion on the actor's part. Mrs. Wallack's vigorous and varied style won her the high praise of a comparison with Mlle George of the Comédie Française, while the verdict of *Le Théâtre* was that, "Mrs. Wallack completely grasped the role of Lady Macbeth and in the sleepwalking scene gave a frightening impression of reality." As we would expect, the final death scene made a profound impression. "One must see Wallack reeling about the stage, his eyes glazing in death, to realize to what a point the depiction of the throes of death can be raised." When we recall the acid comment in 1829 on the death of Rollo in the elder Wallack's *Pizarro*, we recognize that some French critics had certainly changed their opinion with regard to death scenes.

Wallack's next offering was designed to be the ultimate test; on June 25 the company gave *Othello*. The critic of *La Revue des théâtres* was unstinting in his admiration of Shakespeare's power in presenting historical or legendary figures but accorded the ambiguous term "intéressante" to the interpretation. Wallack fell below requirements by his "shouting and undue gesticulation," while Bennett sinned in the opposite direction by playing Iago with disappointing impassivity. Miss Cleveland's Desdemona received the almost standard classification of "touchante." Repenting of his generosity regarding the first evening, M. Dubreuil of *Le Théâtre* was most severe towards *Othello*: "Mr. Wallack," he wrote, "has some very bad habits, among others that of emitting ear-splitting roars.... When Mr. Wallack is alone one can endure it, but when Mr. Bennet also appears it is enough to put one to flight." Apparently the earlier comments on sustained vigour had too much inspired Wallack. A little bewildered by even Miss Cleveland's lustiness, Dubreuil pardoned her because of her beauty. "The rest of the cast," he mournfully concluded, "are very weak."

The strictures were much the same for *Hamlet*, which was played two days later. The critics recognized that Shakespeare had produced a prophetic miracle by creating a sombrely meditative hero during an age of robust action. But, although his comprehension of the role seemed adequate, Wallack's unfortunate trait of constant overemphasis made him unfit to interpret any but violent, agitated scenes. Bennett as Claudius was for some inexplicable reason lacking as was Mrs. Wallack in the role of Gertrude. Ophelia, so difficult to present to a French audience, had a fairly acceptable interpreter in Miss Cleveland. M. Dubreuil of *Le Théâtre*, after promising a discussion of *Hamlet*, later failed to give it.

The descending scale of approval in criticism chimed with public opinion. On the last day of June Mme Ristori, whose performances in the same theatre were creating a furore, encountered a tearful group of young women outside the stage entrance. They were the chorus and performers of the *divertissements* with which Wallack had begun his series. Stranded by the abrupt collapse of the venture they had no resource but charity, which the Italian *prima donna* hastened to extend to them.

Wallack had apparently been promised aid from a London backer; hence the handsome settings and the large and varied personnel of his company. Unfortunately, the backer reneged and of the promised three thousand pounds only five hundred materialized. This reverse, coupled with the listless response of the French public and the deficiencies displayed by the leading players, brought the run to an abrupt close.

Disconcerting as this collapse must have been to most of the participants, one at least apparently did not discard the idea of international dramatic exchange. During the following decade, M. Ruin de Fye intermittently bombarded the government with plans, petitions, *mémoires*, and *exposés*, all calling for the building and promotion of what he styled an Anglo-French theatre.[1] The structure assumed monumental proportions in his plans, seating over five thousand persons and offering the most elaborate productions. M. de Fye pointed out that the *divertissements* offered by the English artists would do away with long intermissions and appealed for the introduction of a great

[1] Alphonse Ruin de Fye, *Théâtre Anglo-Français: Mémoire et plans justificatifs* (Paris, 1861), is the chief of these productions.

foreign dramatic type as a gesture of international goodwill. His outline of personnel called for a dramatic troupe of fifty French players and an English company, which he called a *corps de ballet*, of a hundred, supported by an orchestra of sixty. Apparently, however, M. Ruin de Fye's final appeal in 1863 for a Théâtre International fell on unresponsive departmental ears, and he seems to have abandoned his grandiose ambitions at that point.

Among the *nouvelles diverses* items of the *Revue et gazette des théâtres* for August 30, 1863, appeared a brief note: "The Variétés theatre has just engaged the actor Mathews of the Adelphi theatre, who is to play in an English comedy which he has translated."

Mathews, the son of the comedian Charles Mathews, was a young man, who, in spite of his father's encouragement to go on the stage, had devoted himself to the study of architecture. During a visit to Paris young Mathews had seen and admired the principal French comedians as his father had done shortly before. In 1822 he made an amateur appearance, playing opposite his mother in an adaptation of a French play; in various similar performances he particularly enjoyed playing French characters. Despite his father's urging, he remained with his profession, but continued to dally with dramatics as writer and translator. However, his father's financial collapse in 1833 forced him out of this desultory life into an active career as actor, manager, and author. A further link with French theatre was his marriage in 1838 to Mme Vestris, then manager of the Olympic Theatre. As an actor he could cope only with light comedy works. Fortunately, the roles which he was to play in Paris were in this category and in addition were two of his best interpretations.

The first presentation of the play *Un Anglais timide*, which Mathews himself had translated into French, took place on September 7 and had a far from tranquil *première*. Writing in the *Revue des théâtres* on September 10, Achille Denis reported:

To tell the truth we must say that part of the *Variétés* audiences behaved in a most ungracious manner toward Mr. Mathews. A few finicky people who did not seem to realize the interesting nature of the performance hissed the foreign actor with inexplicable harshness and venom.

M. Denis commented at length on the gracious treatment of French actors in London and also advanced Mathews' claims to consideration both as an established actor and as a man of letters. Apparently many of the audience were in accord with him since he continued: "Let us hasten to add that the hisses were speedily suppressed and that the artists and authors in the hall protested against these unseemly demonstrations."

Apparently the chief difficulty arose from the undue length of the play rather than from Mathews' performance. But the combination of long and complicated farce with a disproportionately heavy role for Mathews proved too much for some less patient auditors, as M. Denis suggests: "Mr. Mathews fills the stage remarkably well, and his role fills the whole play . . . . The play seemed too long and the role ended by becoming boring."

The reviewer for *Le Théâtre* on September 13 recounted Mathews' stage successes, particularly his adaptations from the French. Comparing him to the French actor Arnal, the writer added, "We smile rather than laugh at him. His humour is of a cool description." The public reaction received about the same comment as from *La Revue*: "The public appreciated such qualities. But Mathews' play wearied them. We both commend and condemn them for this."

The justice of these comments was proved by a successful performance on the second evening, after considerable cutting had been done. Reading the lengthy scenario of Mathews' boisterous farce, one sympathizes with the audience at the first presentation. However, Mathews' first night reception irritated his fellow Londoners considerably. *The Daily Telegraph* of September 12, after a lengthy panegyric of Mathews' extremely varied talents, protested that the play had been promptly cut and adapted, and that Mathews had been fulsomely received after the second performance. Descending to the nationalist level, the article averred that the actor's good French and cultivated bearing had disappointed the Parisians, who had looked for the caricature Englishman of the boulevard comedies or of Gustave Doré's humorous drawings.

The *Telegraph* need not have become so incensed, particularly as the newspapers of Paris instituted a veritable campaign on behalf of the visitor. In bidding him farewell on October 11 the *Revue des théâtres* summed up the whole affair very succintly. After announcing that the English actor was obliged to return to London to fill his Haymarket engagement, the writer concluded: "But he will return this winter. Thanks to the press which so ably defended him from the beginning, Charles Mathews will have received justice."

Mr. Mathews did not return that winter, however, but two years later he once again appeared in Paris at another theatre. *Le Théâtre* gave him a flattering introduction in its issue of August 27: "Charles Mathews, the noted English actor, whose talent so closely resembles that of Arnal... is engaged by the Vaudeville for a series of plays." The visitor was to give a French adaptation of *Used Up* under the French title *L'Homme blasé*.

The same journal's initial review of the play on September 7 consisted of a long and cordial discussion of the chief artist's performances.

Mr. Mathews achieved a complete and well merited success. The play is delightful... and the English artist plays his role with remarkable gaiety and naturalness. His French pronunciation is marked by intriguing oddness and an awkwardness which is full of grace.

Good nature is obvious here, but Mathews was also to some degree aided by his role. "The hero whom he represents is a young Englishman overcome with world weariness. If you see the character thus he is well done, and Mr. Mathews has all the capacity required to bring out the comedy and the truth in the character." And so, after further detailed compliments, it is not surprising to read that: "The public gave him the warmest of welcomes and a positive ovation at the close."

The press, however, was not uniformly gentle with Mr. Mathews. Writing late in September, Charles Monselet, quite in the tradition of *Le Courrier des spectacles*, subjected him to a thorough scarifying:

Mr. Charles Mathews has come back to Paris, not to the Variétés this time but to the Vaudeville. Next year he will doubtless make his way to the Gymnase. There are people who seriously take Mr. Mathews to be an actor; I am in a position to assure them that they are wrong. He is a worthy gentleman who regularly takes an annual trip to France to perfect himself in the study (don't say stewdy) of our language. Being quite eccentric, he does not hesitate to ask the public to view his progress: hence these performances or rather exercises, which at first astonished me but to which I am now accustomed. Mr. Mathews learns just one play a year, and then comes to recite it gravely to us until we are tired of it.... This gentleman chooses his exercises with a certain cunning; each of his roles includes a reticence and a halting diction quite in accord with his natural hesitations. A few innocent souls call this natural acting. But let the Vaudeville beware: what with Mme Ristori and Mr. Mathews it is running the risk of being known as a school of gibberish.[2]

---

[2]An unidentified clipping located in the Fonds Rondel, Bibliothèque de l'Arsenal, Paris, erroneously included with material on Charles Mathews Senior.

In spite of this indictment, Mathews terminated his second engagement successfully and returned to London in October.

The end of English "equestrian" influence might be considered to be the French provincial tour of Ducrow in 1819 but there was one remarkable visit nearly fifty years later which deserves notice. The interesting feature in the case concerned was its faithful adherence to the Astley tradition even though the presentation took place on the stage of the Théâtre de la Gaîté.

The year 1867 was marked by the meteoric appearance in Paris of a remarkable woman, Ada Menken, who, though not of English origin, had just come from theatrical activities in London. Born in Louisiana in 1835, Miss Menken in her thirty-three years had had an incredible variety of experiences, ranging from capture by Texas Indians to familiarity with Dickens, Swinburne, Dumas père, and Gautier.

After various attempts at teaching, journalism, and melodramatic acting, Miss Menken discovered her forte in the role of Mazeppa. It is easy to imagine the climax of the drama when the unfortunate hero of Byron's poem lies bound but defiant on the back of the wild horse which is supposed to carry him to lingering death in the wilderness. Miss Menken's American success encouraged her to attempt an appearance as Mazeppa in England. There in October, 1864, at Astley's theatre, she achieved considerable popularity, partly based on a mild succès de scandale (her costume closely approximated that of Gunga Din). For a time at least, as a writer of the period phrased it, "she brought fashionable London across Westminster Bridge."[3] After failing in a somewhat more literary role the following year, Miss Menken proceeded to Paris and took up the equestrian style again.

At the Théâtre de la Gaîté, on December 30, 1866, the melodramatic production *Les Pirates de la Savanne* began a sensational run with Miss Menken as the feminine star creating an absolute furore. Courage must have been needed for this strenuous role but her possession of this is indicated by the fact that when *Mazeppa* had been presented at Astley's Amphitheatre in 1831 a dummy had been used in the wild horse scene. "The chief attraction of the play was the French début of Miss Menken," reported the *Revue et gazette des théâtres*. "She arrived with a reputation as a beauty, a clever pantomimist, and a daring

[3]H. Barton Baker, *The London Stage: Its History and Traditions from 1576 to 1888* (London, 1889; 2 vols.), II, p. 226.

equestrienne." After admitting that she fulfilled the advance publicity, the writer, Maurice Darly, continues:

Her pantomime is lively, sparkling, somewhat Italian. Her courage as an equestrienne is indisputable. They tie her to a bare-backed horse (she is almost equally bare): the horse stamps, bounds, is liberated . . . rushes madly off, rears, leaps the barriers, and climbs to the very rafters at the back.

The production, which had been adapted from an older play, had been enlivened with a Mexican ballet, several scenes based on pseudo American customs and, as a climax, the great Mazeppa tableau. Two months later the play was still the rage of Paris. The knife-throwing duels, the struggles with boa constrictors, and the thrilling Mazeppa scene regularly brought prolonged ovations for the intrepid heroine. The critics lamented that such a superb pantomimist should lack the ability to speak French. An actress capable of expressing joy, grief, indignation, and gaiety with such vividness could, in their opinion, rival the best Parisian artists.

Such was the length of run envisaged for the play that the manager of the Gaîté had to face official complaints from two playwrights whose work was being denied production. By arrangement these two gentlemen were allowed 5 per cent of the author's royalties for every subsequent performance of Miss Menken. By April 7 months more of success were prophesied, particularly because of an "Exposition Universelle" which was to be held in Paris that year. However, the manager of the Gaîté received bad news shortly after. Miss Menken had signed a contract to appear at a Viennese theatre; despite frantic appeals by the Gaîté, she was obliged to abide by it, the only concession being a few supplementary performances before her departure. Her final appearances aroused general ovations. Even M. Listener, the august literary critic of the *Revue des théâtres*, wrote: "As for Miss Menken, she is applauded and called back by the crowds, charmed as they are by her lively pantomiming, her expressive face, and the daring grace of her actions." The Mazeppa episode he still found "an unexpected and gripping scene." After over a hundred performances *Les Pirates* was finally replaced in May.

Such success was considered good justification for a new engagement the following year. But this was not destined to be filled. While rehearsing the next year for a revival of her celebrated Mazeppa role in Paris, Miss Menken died and was buried in the city of her triumphs.

The Franco-British exchange of artists had certainly an occasional touch of the ludicrous. The theatrical career of Miss Cora Pearl at the Bouffes Parisiens in January, 1867, is a good example. A well-known demi-mondaine of the period, Miss Pearl was born Elizabeth Cronch in Liverpool. She had spent a considerable part of her twenty-five years in Paris, managing to retain, however, a very distinct English accent. At the beginning of 1867 the manager of the Bouffes, faced with a theatrical slump and a hoarse leading lady, in desperation appealed to Miss Pearl to sing the role of Cupidon in Offenbach's *Orphée aux Enfers*. Miss Pearl accepted with what was apparently characteristic brashness and, after hasty but strenuous priming, began what she herself describes as a whimsical handling of the role. For some reason the critic of *La Revue et gazette des théâtres* chose to take her début as being a serious attempt to begin a stage career. "At the risk of being laughed at," he wrote, "we propose to say a few words about an effort which looks frivolous but which perhaps reveals a secret desire of Miss Cora's to direct her life in a more serious way and to gain by means of work a respite from the weariness of pleasure." He proceeded to disclose the shams of her performance with deadly accuracy, detecting her hasty preparation, her imperfect memorization of theatrical tricks, and her faulty interpretation. With the rest of the audience he was profoundly jarred by her English accent, especially in her singing. He concluded with a warning to the would-be artist, "She would be mistaken to take seriously the noisy and partly ironic reception which her many friends have given her."

The critic need scarcely have exerted himself; Miss Pearl's career lasted twelve nights and that length was largely owing to managerial determination, staunch efforts of an energetic claque, and the patience of the general public. The English accent, however, finally proved too much for the audience, and the hapless Cora was hissed off the stage. In her memoirs she reports, with her customary candour, that she went on the stage without any desire and left it without any regrets.[4] To judge from other sources of information the lack of regret was universal. On February 10 we read again from the critic of *La Revue et gazette des théâtres*: "Miss Cora Pearl has given up the stage. The calling of this improvised artist could not resist the hisses which greeted her these last few days. Let us hope that the public will not yearn unduly for Miss Cora."

[4] Cora Pearl, *Memoirs* (Paris, 1886; 2 vols.), I, *passim* for this incident.

Late in June, 1867, Parisian walls were sprinkled with advertisements in which appeared the portrait of a gentleman chiefly notable for an impressive pair of side-whiskers. The actor thus announced was Edward Sothern, whose career up to that date hae been a chequered one. On July 7 *La Revue et gazette des théâtres* carried the following brief note among its *Variétés*: "Tomorrow Mr. Sothern will play at the Théâtre Impérial Italien the role of Lord Dundreary in the comedy *American Cousin* [sic]. An outstanding success is anticipated."

Entering the theatrical profession in 1849 Sothern had barely maintained his position as a utility player (indeed, during a brief American tour in the early fifties, he lost his place from sheer incompetence). None the less, he persisted in the profession, gaining experience with various stock companies, until in 1858 he assumed the role in which he became famous. Sothern gradually enlarged the small part of the vapid Lord Dundreary in *Our American Cousin* by including amusing foibles, eccentricities, and droll comments. Finally, with this character of his own creation, he reappeared in London in 1861 where he suddenly caught public fancy and became the rage of the capital. The play ran for almost five hundred nights and provoked all manner of imitations, from wearing special waistcoats to cultivating the famous side-whiskers with which the character became permanently associated. Capitalizing on his success, Sothern produced two other plays centring round the Dundreary figure, which became increasingly extravagant but remained consistently popular.

On July 12 Desgranges of *La Revue des théâtres* reviewed the production.

Here is Sothern in Paris with a complete company. What luck for the English in Paris and even for the Parisians who in their turn are going to see Lord Dundreary and be in a position to appreciate such a highly regarded actor, not to mention the fact that *Cousin from America* [sic] offers us a curious example of the contemporary English theatre.

The critic remarked that Sothern and his role were almost synonymous and made the obvious comparison with the case of Lemaître and *Robert Macaire*. "The role of Lord Dundreary," he continued, "hardly constitutes a part of the play, but it does form a highly amusing episode, and this role which Sothern conceived and built up ... has made his fortune." After a lengthy résumé of the play, which concerns the adventures of a brash young American in England, the critic described Lord Dundreary:

A vague being, absent-minded and never in touch with things, Sothern plays the part delightfully. One can scarcely imagine the coolness and dry comedy which he shows in this amusing creation. He remains imperturbable in the midst of the most uproarious scenes... he talks, chatters, gets utterly lost, flounders hilariously.

Obviously, the visitors could hardly have asked for a more understanding and sympathetic critic. He recognized that many of the untranslatable verbal jugglings and outlandish sallies of the comedy had inevitably eluded the French listeners. But, in spite of that, he maintained: "It is a very curious spectacle, but one of real interest; and we hope that Sothern will be as cordially applauded in Paris as he has been in England." M. Desgranges also made approving reference to Miss Rose Massey as the heroine and to Mr. Raymond as the American cousin. The latter might be expected to feel at home in his part since he was a well-known American comedian. Unfortunately, the public did not share the critic's enthusiasm, for the Paris run was neither very long nor very successful. Sothern had tended to give his role an increasingly exaggerated and extravagant interpretation. This quality of caricature added to the difficulties of the play in general and apparently proved too much for the Parisians; after a run of less than three weeks, the company withdrew.

A member of the troupe, not mentioned but destined to greater fame than any of the others, was a young man of twenty-nine, already a veteran of ten years' varied trouping. He was Henry Irving, who played the role of Abel Murcatt in his single professional visit to Paris. However, the visit exerted a genuine influence upon the great actor's career. Irving remained in Paris during August and assiduously attended the theatres despite his limited French. He watched with profound admiration the artists of the Comédie Française, particularly the wonderful comedian Coquelin. Their evident mastery of theatrical techniques, their confident reliance on a long and gracious theatrical inheritance made young Irving realize the fragmentary nature of his apprenticeship. "At the Comédie Française," writes a recent biographer, "he discovered a style of play-acting and of dramatic writing which, with all its superb technical accomplishments, sprang directly from the genius of Molière."[5] He indulged in no jealousy or self-abasement, but rather was grateful for this revelation of the art which he adored.

[5] Laurence Irving, *Henry Irving* (London, 1951), p. 139.

12 · Here Come the Clowns!

Among the most popular features of Astley's pre-Revolution productions in France were the clowns. These were not the *pagliacci* of the Italian troupes nor the *paillasses* as the French at first called them. The French themselves recognized the difference by accepting along with the English comics their own English name. The clown's varied ancestry probably includes the buffoons of mediaeval farces and interludes, the court jester of later days, the *gracioso* of Spanish comedies, the Italian Pierrot, and the fools of Shakespeare. His appearance in pantomime came relatively late in France, where Harlequin long remained the popular figure. It can, in fact, be reasonably argued that, like the equestrian virtuoso, the clown was an import from Britain which the French slowly accepted and were later able to equal among their own artists. "France has produced a few famous clowns such as Auriol and Mazurier," remarks Henri Frichet, "but the clown has remained an English specialty, distinctively English because he personifies that extraordinary tendency toward eccentricity which is the dominant symptom of Anglo-Saxon melancholy."[1]

The first British clown to appear in France belonged to Astley's troupe. Billy Saunders by name, he headed a considerable body of clowns but stood quite above them in talent. Nougaret tells us that the equestrian performances at Astley's were "enlivened by the buffooneries of a very clever *paillasse*." This pioneer originated a variety of items, which later appeared in his successors' repertoires. He presented a group of trained dogs, foreshadowing many animal acts, and also began the use of English-French jargon in which the humour of the speeches was enhanced by atrocious mispronunciation and an exaggerated English accent. In addition, Saunders frequently played as an equestrian comic in the pantomimes, while the general clown troupe appeared some mounted, some on foot. So great was their popularity that pressure was exerted by the French manager Nicolet, and the

[1] Henri Frichet, *Le Cirque et les Forains* (Paris, 1898), p. 82.

police ordered the clowns out of the ring. Astley at once obeyed the letter of the law in a surprising fashion. The English comedian Decastro, in his *Memoirs*, tells how the equestrian impresario

caused a number of horses to be harnessed and tackled together as one solid body or as so many well-driven piles that he was enabled to raise a platform stage to rest on their backs in a firm steady manner by which means he accomplished his evasion of the police, to the great discomfiture of M. Nicolai, as on that plan his performance was still but horsemanship, and the ingenuity of M. Astley was most liberally rewarded by the people of Paris, natives as well as resident strangers of all nations on that occasion.[2]

This remarkable arrangement is illustrated by a contemporary print in which sixteen stout horses carry the clowns' platform.

Astley's clowns and horses also performed in combination to give comic interludes and pantomimes. One of these, "The Tailor and his Horse," became a classic in the early nineteenth-century Paris circuses. The hapless tailor in the pantomime buys a savage mount which attacks him instantly and pursues him over and through a series of obstacles. It is easily seen that such a little pantomime would require a highly acrobatic clown and a highly trained horse. In a small volume, *Le Cirque Olympique*, which describes the Franconi establishment as it existed about 1817, one of the engravings represents a *paillasse* whose act was obviously largely equestrian. The writer comments approvingly on the daring feats of horsemanship displayed and adds: "Two comic scenes usually act as the interlude between the displays of strength and skill."[3] One of these scenes was none other than "The Tailor and his Horse" and the other was a scene featuring a peasant Claune, who encountered similar mishaps with a horse. There is no question that Astley's clowns began a long and vital tradition of British participation in comic circus entertainment in France.

When, after his brilliant season of equestrian and pantomime performances at Franconi's, the great Ducrow returned to England in 1819, he did so largely to recruit reinforcements in the persons of three comics, Garthwaeth, Derwin, and Blanchard, in order to ensure his success in *The Magic Tomb*. These performers were not merely clowns but leading members of a pantomime troupe and their model was the great pantomimist of Drury Lane, Joe Grimaldi. The clown in the modern circus sense of the word did not appear until the middle of the

[2] J. Decastro, *The Memoirs of J. D. Comedian* (London, 1824), p. 124.
[3] Mme B__xx__ née de V__xx__, *Le Cirque Olympique* (Paris, 1817), pp. 37–8.

century. Only in the early days of the Second Empire were the first modern clowns to be seen in Paris; throughout the first half of the century the visiting clowns participated as theatrical performers in pantomime productions.

An interesting figure in this category appeared in Paris the year following Ducrow's season. He was Clement Philippe Laurent, whose father, a French pantomimist and *joueur de marionnettes*, had been brought to England by Philip Astley. Laurent had appeared in Paris in 1818-19 at the Théâtre de la Gaîté, presenting an acrobatic act with his brother Charles. He had higher ambitions, however, and in 1821 he returned to the French capital. There he joined the theatre of the Funambules (tightrope walkers), the popular *théâtre à quatre sous*, where Debureau, the pantomime artist, reigned so long as Pierrot. In *Le Théâtre des Funambules*, Péricaud states: "The public had noticed two years previously at the Théâtre de la Gaîté . . . two English clowns, the Laurent brothers, who by their acrobatic eccentricities, their incredible contortions, and their dazzling balancing acts achieved very great success."[4] These two brothers, "just arrived from England," were naturally assigned to the acrobatic section. Knowing no French, they resolutely began to learn the language although their performance did not require it.

The brothers were shortly transferred to the Funambules theatre, that is, to the pantomime section, and here they found their permanent positions in close collaboration with Debureau. The younger Laurent played the second Pierrot roles after Debureau's lead. The elder, a man of more notable artistic stature, developed as his specialty the character of Harlequin. He was supple, graceful, and an excellent dancer, and his success threatened to eclipse Debureau's. The rivalry between them finally culminated in fisticuffs; after that the two artists, recognizing that they were really complementary to each other, decided to collaborate for mutual success.

As well as acting, Laurent soon developed remarkable capacities as a stage manager. His English background had given him a wide acquaintanceship with all the procedures of the *pantomime anglaise* and in particular the special stage effects and transformation scenes so common in British pantomime. These he imported and adapted in such quantity that he became known as *l'Homme Truc*.

[4] L. Péricaud, *Le Théâtre des funambules* (Paris, 1897), pp. 46 ff.

In 1827 Laurent produced a pantomime *Le Bœuf Enragé*, which set a record at the Funambules by its phenomenal popularity and also by its influence on subsequent productions. Péricaud suggests half-humorously that: "Debureau and Laurent were founding a school as were Hugo and Delacroix. Laurent was producing *Le Bœuf Enragé* just as Hugo was creating *Hernani* and Delacroix *The Death of Sardanapalus*."[5] Indeed it was in *Le Bœuf Enragé* that Debureau made his first notable impression. The pantomime became a perennial feature of the theatre and, over ten years later, Laurent transferred some of the scenes from it to the even more famous production of *Les Pilules du Diable* at Franconi's.

The Funambules attracted not merely the *petit bourgeois* but also a considerable number of intellectuals. Among these Charles Nodier, of whimsical talent, became so intrigued with pantomimes that he wrote one himself. *Le Songe d'Or*, which ran for hundreds of nights to full houses, bore the subtitle *pantomime anglaise*, and Nodier insisted that Laurent should be in complete charge of the production. Various critics have described it as among the best works of the kind ever written. Nodier refused to acknowledge his authorship in order, as his friends suggested, that he might praise it; this he frequently did, in warm terms. Though Laurent was producer of *Le Songe d'Or*, Debureau carried the leading role and gathered fresh fame from it.

Through the early and middle thirties Laurent remained with the Funambules. His name appeared with diminishing frequency as a member of the cast but his work as producer absorbed an increasing amount of his time. An amusing episode in 1836 indicates that the French still considered his connections with his native land to be of some significance. The theatre was threatened with closure on account of the misbehaviour of two of its actors on the stage and the desperate management despatched Laurent to interview the English ambassador in an attempt to enlist his support on their behalf. No record remains of the actor's reception at the embassy. Happily the matter was soon arranged by the manager's personal intervention.

In 1838 Laurent left his brother to continue playing Pierrot at the Funambules and went to the Franconi circus. His most famous production, *Les Pilules du Diable*, filled houses for the managers of the Cirque Olympique for many years. With his new employers he continued to

[5] *Ibid.*, p. 69.

exercise his special talents as author and as stage director for over a decade.

The gifts of this artist were especially important in shaping the pantomime at the Funambules. Among the various collaborators of the great Debureau, Beaulieu, in his work on the popular theatres, places at the head of the list, "The elder Laurent, an English pantomimist, author of many pantomimes, and a brilliant producer."[6]

A brief but financially successful appearance in Paris is referred to in the verbose, though unrewarding, journal of the veteran English pantomime clown, Old Barnes. Writing in *Bentley's Miscellany* in 1830, he makes a passing reference to a Paris visit in 1825 with Tom Ellar. Apparently no great impression was made on the French critics.

In 1826, Parsloe, a highly successful and typical example of the pantomime clown, appeared at the Porte-Saint-Martin theatre. He had made his début during the latter portion of Thomas Cooke's engagement in *Le Monstre et le Magicien*, and for a time the two British artists dominated the stage at that theatre. Parsloe headed a group of English clowns, but among the elaborate settings and overwhelming stage effects the players, except for Parsloe himself and the Frenchman Mazurier who played opposite him, were largely submerged. Connecting the attraction with *Le Monstre*, a French critic remarked: "After having shuddered, we are now going to laugh English style." The pantomime, entitled *Scaramouche*, was really an adaptation of the old Don Juan *Festin de Pierre* theme, "arranged English fashion, that is with elaborate sets and highly diverting acrobatics." The opening was delayed a few days by an accident in which Parsloe injured his leg in a stage trap-door. But on August 19 *Scaramouche* was warmly received at its *première*. When one considers the vitriolic comments of *Le Courrier des théâtres* on English actors in general, it is interesting to read its announcement of the performance on August 18.

The chief role in this British farce will be carried by Mr. Parsloe (pronounced Pazelot) who is described as amazing in this field. ... In line with our national taste we will laugh at a spectacle intended merely to amuse us. When it is a question of interpreting *Tartuffe* that will be another matter.

Parsloe's popularity increased steadily as he skilfully combined with his French colleagues and adapted his style and matter to French tastes. By carefully emphasizing and developing the distinctively

[6] Henri de Beaulieu, *Les Théâtres du boulevard du crime* (Paris, 1905), p. 138.

English elements in his presentation which had pleased the crowds, he attained "un succès complet," high praise from French quarters. During the month's visit Parsloe appeared nearly thirty times, the few breaks being occasioned by various benefit performances. When, a few days after Cooke had returned to England, the jovial pantomimist also embarked for London, the following comment appeared: "M. Parsloe is on the Calais-Dover boat. No new English imports are announced."

The following year (1827-8) three more clown-pantomimists appeared in Paris at the Cirque Olympique. Southey (a brother of the poet) and Blanchard, who had visited France in 1819, joined with Ellar in various acts. Their run, although extending over nearly a year, could not have been very successful as they are featured on the Franconi billings in the *Courrier des théâtres* only at widely separated intervals, with long breaks when presumably they were not with the company at all. Their total of some forty appearances during this time does not compare strikingly with that of several other performers, particularly the French version of the circus clown, the *grotesque*.

The *grotesque*, a posturing buffoon in the Italian tradition, remained the French circus clown until he was replaced in the fifties by the more clever and original British and Spanish performers. His theatrical equivalent was the Pierrot of the *Funambules*. Debureau had greatly developed and popularized this rather unlikeable Italian figure by making his Pierrot more human and relating him to contemporary social types, frequently with effects of parody or satire. As early as 1832, however, Jules Janin, commenting on Debureau's rivals, wrote: "The English clowns have brought all Paris to see them; their offerings stood up to the scrutiny of the loges and the rivalry of one of the best orchestras in France."[7]

Among these English visitors we discover Old Barnes, who had briefly visited France with Ellar in 1825. Volume VII of *Bentley's Miscellany* (1830) contains lengthy extracts from this famous Pantaloon's so-called Journal, referred to above, which centres around a meandering narrative of his visit to Paris in May and June of 1830. His account of the journey from London to Paris is amusingly detailed, with comments on sea-sickness and foreign food, and also on French postillions, and the tense political atmosphere in France. According to his own version Barnes was loftily announced: "Role de Pantaloon par

[7] Jules Janin, *Histoire du théâtre à quatre sous* (Paris, 1832; 2 vols.), I, p. 120.

Monsieur Barnes première artist [sic] des Théâtres Royales [sic] de Londres." He found French audiences to his liking, and commented on the good order maintained in French theatres, where the pranks of English crowds were not, according to him, permitted. "No," he writes, "the people behaved better to both actors and authors; and if a person happens to be pertinaciously troublesome in any way, he is invited out of the theatre by a gensd'arme [sic] in a uniform somewhat like that worn by the Oxford Blues in Dighton's time."[8] Unfortunately the visitor dismisses the month of June with the exasperatingly brief entry: "Excitement of acting during the remainder of the month."

In July his attention, and that of the rest of Paris, was directed to political events by the three-day revolution which ended the reign of Charles X. This event he saw at a discreet distance, and his comments on it are both lengthy and interesting. The journal concludes at this point, indicating that he left Paris immediately afterward, apparently without resuming his theatrical performances.

During the thirties English clowns do not seem to have appeared in France. Various reasons for this may be suggested. In England the popularity of the pantomime gave these performers good scope for their talents at home. Furthermore, France was well supplied with its own entertainers: Debureau was coming to the pinnacle of his popularity; Mazurier held high favour; and the brilliant Auriol, after many years of absence abroad, returned to make his début at the Cirque Olympique. Jean Gontard proved so good as an acrobatic clown that the Astley family brought him to their London Amphitheatre in 1838. Also, from 1830 on, the Franconi amphitheatre launched a series of spectacular *mimo-drames* in which the grandiose tended to submerge the comic. These continued until nearly 1850 before the public began to weary of them.

After the death of Grimaldi in 1837 something of a crisis overtook the English pantomime and its clowns. The temporary decline in popularity of the pantomime drove its chief actors into other fields. Some managed to maintain their places in the theatres as broad comedians; a great number migrated to the circus and, as this field became overcrowded, many moved to the Continent. Here the demand was steady, and since the reputation of English clowns was high, the average Continental circus relied on carrying a troupe of clowns, half

[8] *Bentley's Miscellany* (London, 1838), VII, p. 457.

of whom would be British. Also, the steady rise in the popularity and number of Parisian permanent circuses in the last half of the century helped to make the French capital a Mecca for dispossessed English Harlequins.

It is impossible to identify all the expatriates who invaded the Continent. The only names remaining are of those who made some distinctive advance in technique or some notable addition to the clowns' repertoire. Fleeting reference to a group of unusually adept stilt walkers, brief mention of an equestrian who missed connections with his mount and was carried out but appeared later smiling bravely, a comparison of some new acrobat to the master Auriol: these are the only survivals of the vast majority of the *clowns anglais* who travelled across Europe at this period.

An innovation at this time was the fact that some clowns remained in France for periods of years. Commenting on the various types of circus contract Strehly writes: "When they have attained a certain popularity, clowns are hired by the year and some of them become pillars of the establishments."[9] A few clowns played back and forth between the two countries; but those who were genuinely successful in Paris usually remained there until they finished their career or until they left France permanently.

The eighteen forties may then be considered as a period of transition from the older pantomime clown to the circus performer. Two names adequately represent the two types: Tom Mathews and Thomas Kemp. Mathews continued the tradition of bringing to the French stage a complete English pantomime. With the elaborateness which had developed in the English pantomime productions, this involved heavy risks. A full company and all the costly and cumbrous equipment required for the impressive transformation effects had to be imported; apparently Mathews was the only English pantomimist to have undertaken such an ambitious venture. In the summer of 1842, Nestor Roqueplan, manager of the Variétés, arranged with Mathews to import an English troupe for the presentation of the pantomime *Harlequin Chasseur*. "Everything is English in the pantomime which the Théâtre des Variétés is bringing us," reported *Les Coulisses*, "the dancers, the clowns, the settings, even the music; the terms of the engagement are also English, that is to say very stiff." In fact, M.

[9] G. Strehly, *L'Acrobatie et les Acrobates* (Paris, 1903), p. 58.

Roqueplan engaged himself for the sum of eighty thousand francs in addition to special benefit performances.

The pantomime opened late in July and proved very successful even to the *Coulisses* critic, who gave it the honour of a report on August 7. Under the title "Harlequin, a pantomime based on kicks," he wrote: "The kick forms the basis of all burlesque pantomime and this familiar but expressive gesture is known in every land . . . and strange as it may seem it always raises a laugh." Quite prepared to judge the work on that basis, he continues: "The Harlequin at the Variétés has maintained all his good habits and has followed the best traditions of his forefathers; and as ever his sallies, his surprise transformations, and his splits have brought merriment." As is so frequently the case in these circumstances, the critic felt bound to suggest that the play bore a strong resemblance to a French work, in this instance to the standby of the Franconi stage, *Les Pilules du Diable*. With memories of exactly twenty years before in mind, he comments on the contrast between the somewhat strained political atmosphere between the two countries and the reciprocity of cordiality on the stage. "Without wishing to compare the clown Mathews to Bouffé, we are happy to see this kindly welcome to English players after the applause which has just been lavished on our artists of the Théâtre Français in London." Unknown to the critic an international link also existed in the person of one of the clowns. A junior member of the troupe, James Flexmore, was a few years later to become the son-in-law of the great Auriol. The French comedian had married an English girl and their eldest child, Francesca, became Flexmore's wife. A talented and imaginative performer, Flexmore was one of Grimaldi's most gifted successors in England; the visit of 1842 was his only one to France.

It is amusing to note a few days later among the *Petites Nouvelles* a partisan squib on the political plane intended for home consumption. "Comedy is a mirror. Yesterday three cabinet ministers at the Théâtre des Variétés saw themselves in action as they watched the clowns."

On the second Sunday of the engagement M. Roqueplan, deciding that the weather was too hot for a performance, announced a *relâche*. A large crowd had gathered and some imaginative person launched the rumour that there was an objection among the troupe to playing on Sunday. This led to a considerable riot. Thus, a wheel had come full circle: twenty years before, almost to the date, Penley's English actors had caused a riot by proposing to play in Paris.

Not all the reactions to the Mathews group were favourable, as the comments of Paul Hugounet, a passionate amateur of French pantomime, illustrate. Writing years later in 1889, he says of English pantomime in general that it was too violent for French taste. Although he admits that Mathews' production was an attempt to revive the traditional Italian pantomime, he declares it to have been a failure, all the more marked because the artists were of good quality.

M. Hugounet's recollections are inaccurate as to the date of the visit and also as to the theatre concerned. None the less, his attitude is familiar in that it represented a recoil from something which he considered extreme and artistically unacceptable.[10]

The performances continued for somewhat less than the month intended. On Thursday, August 18, just three weeks after the opening of the pantomime, another play appeared on the bills.

Whatever M. Roqueplan's feelings may have been, Mathews could not have retained any unfavourable memories of Paris, for he returned in the summer of 1853 to the Porte-Saint-Martin theatre. The presentation was a traditional pantomime, *Harlequin Hudibras*, in which Mathews himself played both of the chief roles. In the eighteenth-century tradition the English production provided the *divertissement* for a highly successful drama, *L'Honneur de la maison*, both performances opening on the same night. Describing the visitors as the "famous pantomimist Mathews and other English artists," the critic Saint Agnan Choler remarked on the popularity of the farce *Hudibras* in England. He recognized that it would inevitably lose some of its appeal in France but "it will retain enough humour, enough surprises, enough acrobatic tricks and sufficient new dancing to rouse our curiosity." The same writer, discussing the opening performance on July 20, characterized the production as a mixture of traditional pantomime and English adaptation.

> You would fancy yourself at the Funambules and would be wallowing in reminiscences but for the national character of this genuinely English spectacle. The action is splendid; it is the type of action made famous by Debureau. But what differs basically is the appearance of the actors.

---

[10] P. Hugounet, *Mimes et Pierrots* (Paris, 1889), p. 195.

Conventional as the characters they played might be, these English interpreters gave them an appealing novelty to French eyes.

There is a clown who in his grimaces displays the finest comic; a wonderfully wooden Pantaloon; a Columbine as graceful as can be, and a Harlequin full of suppleness and agility.

The critic concludes by suggesting that the general lustiness of the English presentation had pleased the audience.

But, as with the earlier visit, there were reservations in more thoughtful quarters. In his essay *De l'essence du rire*, Charles Baudelaire refers at considerable length to the Mathews production.

I shall long remember the first English pantomime that I saw. It was at the Variétés a few years ago. Few will recall it probably for very few people seemed to care for that type of entertainment and the poor English pantomimists received a very poor welcome among us.[11]

He attributed the lack of appeal to national differences, especially the exaggerated violence of the English artists. "The English Pierrot," he stated, "comes in like a whirlwind ... and when he laughs he makes the hall shake." Referring to the garish costumes and make-up, he continued: "Everything was similarly exaggerated in this strange play; it showed the giddiness of hyperbole." Yet he admitted realism of a macabre kind in the acting. "Because of the peculiar talent of English actors for hyperbole, all these monstrous farces take on a strangely gripping reality." When one recalls the marked taste for the macabre, even the gruesome which Baudelaire displayed in his work, and his admiration of Edgar Allen Poe these comments are rather surprising. Perhaps the tendency developed at a later date. In any case, the macabre in Baudelaire's work is directed to a tragic end and not a comic as with the clowns.

On August 11 it was reported that: "*L'Honneur de la Maison* ... and the English ballet with Mathews and his Company are honourably holding the stage and still attracting the public." Finally, on August 26, both productions were withdrawn to make way for an extravaganza which the management of the Porte-Saint-Martin had been preparing for some time. Mathews' was the last visit of the traditional English pantomime clown to France. In its nature, its position as *divertissement*,

[11] Charles Baudelaire, *Oeuvres complètes* (Paris, 1882; 4 vols.), II, pp. 379 ff.

and its varied reception his appearance can be said to represent completely the pantomime visits.

Thomas Kemp, the second intermediate figure, is considerably important in the story of the British clown in France because he marked the transition from a pantomime performer in the older sense, that is, a performer in a theatrical production, to a clown in the circus sense of the word, that is, a presenter of acrobatic juggling, *lazzi*, and short unconnected drolleries in the ring. It is true that Kemp did appear at the Cirque Olympique, but he began his performances there by taking part in representations which were described on the bills not only as pantomimes but also as *pantomimes italiennes* occasionally. His brilliantly coloured, closely-fitting costume recalled the Italian type of clown to the audiences. Kemp's early appearances in 1853 were not especially popular with the French, partly because he was playing in the old Italian vehicle which was losing its appeal, but more particularly because some of his solo numbers were too strange to the onlookers. Like Parsloe in the twenties, however, he had the ingenuity to adapt his presentations to please the Parisians without sacrificing their English quality. His performances at the Cirque de l'Impératrice in May 1853 won the approval of his audiences: "Kemp, the English clown, regularly amuses the public, who have taken him into favour."

Among the performers on this occasion was the ever-popular Auriol, and in the audience, Napoleon III and Eugénie. Two months later the comedians were again praised. "As for the clowns and especially Kemp, nothing could be more amusing than the tricks that they invent and carry out every night before a packed house."

In July the circus was able to draw crowds despite the hot weather so feared by entertainment managers.

For has the circus not assembled the most complete collection possible of first class clowns, which alone are worth the price of admission? At their head the veteran Auriol . . . his son Baptiste as Pierrot; Kemp, who is so whimsical and amusing; and finally Candler and Laristi, who are so daring.

This array of talent is very interesting. Auriol figured essentially as a nimble acrobat rather than as a clown; his son carried on the Italian tradition. Kemp was eccentric, while Candler and Laristi, an international team, introduced a fresh element into the acrobatics. After announcing further startling aerial performances from the Candler-

Laristi team, the report concluded: "While awaiting this marvellous performance let us recommend the highly amusing pantomime *The Enchanted Tree* to be followed by an interlude." Again old and new are juxtaposed.

In his successive seasons in Paris, Kemp won his place as an excellent comedian with the clown troupe and in solo numbers. He also left many marks of the English clown on the French circus. Most obvious was the lurid make-up which is now naturally associated with the billowing costume and disordered wig of the clown but which in the "land of the pale-faced Pierrot" appeared a startling and grotesque novelty. A reasonably good acrobat and a skilful juggler, Kemp was appealing largely because of his whimsical humour which the French recognized as distinctive and for which they developed a certain liking. In *Le Théâtre* of June, 1855, Kemp was flatteringly compared with another artist. Referring to a daring tightrope walker, the reviewer stated, "We unhesitatingly prefer Kemp's agility." Kemp's career was unfortunately terminated in 1855 because of his alcoholic excesses. In June of that year crowds and critics were admiring "the antics of Kemp," and a short time later we find another tribute to "the convulsing Kemp." Within a few months he was dead.

Boswell, who became Kemp's chief successor as *clown anglais* at the Cirque de l'Impératrice, appeared with him for some time before his death. In fact, Boswell had been appearing for at least three years in Paris when he was called upon to take the place of his popular fellow clown. He too had achieved considerable public favour by two or three specialities. At a time when the typical circus clown was an acrobat *par excellence*, Boswell developed a number of aerial acts which have defied repetition. He made his Paris début in 1853 in the difficult act, "l'homme renversé," which received the comment, "Nothing can excel his acts from the point of view of acrobatics." His performances later in the season evoked more praise. "The new English clown is performing wonders at the Cirque Napoléon as he did at the Champs Elysées: each evening he produces more new tricks." The most celebrated of his gymnastic feats bore the title "l'Echelle cassée." Climbing a ladder held upright in the air by a fellow clown, Boswell discarded each rung as he mounted. When he reached the top he discarded one of the sides and proceeded to balance head down on the remaining side. He also used a troupe of trained dogs, one of which,

Roland by name, was hailed by one reporter as a new clown. He was, finally, a genuinely comic performer when he wished, with a humour more robust than Kemp's but highly effective with French audiences. In 1859, in a discussion of the English clown, Maurice Sand, after expressing his amazement at the costume and make-up of that "strange and fantastic being," continued:

> His behaviour is as singular as his costume; he is not silent like our Pierrot, on the contrary he carries on with ridiculous conversation and is in addition an experienced comic acrobat. Kemp, who died a few years ago, and Boswell, both circus clowns, are examples of this type. One cannot watch Boswell without admiring his strength and skill or without bursting with laughter at his odd and varied comicalities.[12]

Boswell, much more so than Kemp, corresponded to the conventional conception of the melancholy British clown. In spite of his hilarious tricks he had about him something disturbingly macabre. Before his death in 1859, this strange being, who quoted Shakespeare through luridly painted lips, completed the introduction of the *clown britannique* to Paris.

With Boswell came a whole group of acrobat clowns, each displaying some special talent in addition to the routine displays of agility. Appearing on the bills as early as 1841, Candler performed with a French associate Laristi in the most daring aerial acrobatics, even walking head downwards on the interior of the tent roof at the Cirque d'Eté. He held his place for years among the best of both French and British performers before retiring from his hazardous profession to engage in trade in England. William Wheal, a close imitator of Boswell, in addition to being a superb acrobat, also presented pantomimed parodies, including one of *Hamlet* which must have been an odd item but which became a standard in the clown repertoire. These men pursued their careers throughout the fifties.

In the middle of the decade also appeared the Price brothers, with a fresh attraction. Their act was a combination of acrobatics and music; mounted on two ladders which they maintained in delicate equilibrium they played a duet on violin and flute. Really not clowns at all (in the sense of broad comics), the Prices during more than ten years of popularity distinguished themselves as graceful equilibrists and encouraged many imitators. Speaking of John Price, M. Rémy thus characterized him: "He scorned speech. Slight, precise, reserved, and

[12]Maurice Sand, *Masques et Bouffons* (Paris, 1860; 2 vols.), II, p. 297.

methodical, he personified the impassive British clown."[18] Their imitators undoubtedly found the grace and dexterity of the brothers easier to comprehend than the more robust or boisterous elements of other British performers. And the fact that the Prices as has been mentioned completely eschewed speech and played in a cool impassive fashion certainly encouraged French imitations of their techniques.

Chadwick, the least original of the main group, distinguished himself by the length of his career in Paris, rather than by any particular virtuosity. Appearing for the first time in 1863 at the Cirque d'Hiver and the Cirque d'Eté, he joined the leading English and French clowns in the farcical interludes which Wheal and others had developed. As a junior performer in the troupe he often played the role of the unwanted person in a party, the importunate nuisance, thus foreshadowing a very important member of the clown family. Chadwick's chief contribution was his long term as ring-master of the Nouveau Cirque, a responsibility which he assumed when that establishment was founded and which he held until his death in 1889.

Our study of clowns has brought us to the later years of the Second Empire in France. Throughout the period covered there had been a great development in the world of the clown, but more striking changes were still to come.

[18]Tristan Rémy, *Les Clowns* (Paris, 1945), p. 51.

13 · Tumblers and Talkers, a Fool and Footitt

In the Second Empire a notable change in the career of the clown had occurred in his departure from the theatre for the sawdust ring. This period saw the introduction and acceptance of the British clown who displaced the *grotesque*, and the development of various specialized forms of clowning all of which had in common acrobatic skill. But the clown in the form popularized by these earlier figures no longer commanded public favour after 1870. In the following twenty years, three major developments took place in the evolution of the clown in France, each introduced and dominated by British performers.

The first of these was the development of the acrobatic pantomime, with which the names of the Hanlon-Lee troupe are inseparably linked. The six Hanlons had made their first appearance in England before the middle of the century, specializing in aerial acrobatics under the direction of Lee, whose skill as a gymnast was equalled by his acumen as a promoter. After a passing appearance at the Paris Hippodrome in 1848, the company sought more lucrative fields in America. Here in 1855 they encountered the French pantomimist Agoust, and began a new type of entertainment, the acrobatic pantomime. Finally, in 1867, their second French appearance took place at the Cirque d'Hiver. Although they had made no attempt at originality in the plot of their so-called pantomime, their new technique of combining acrobatics and pantomime appealed to the public. The war of 1870 forced them to return to England until 1872, when they appeared in five acts at the Folies Bergère.[1]

Their next, and outstanding, appearance came in the autumn of 1878 at the Variétés, where they began an impressive run of thirteen months. Their opening production, *Do, sol, mi, do*, consisted of a ferocious parody of an orchestra rehearsal in which everything breakable was reduced to fragments. Their second item, the famous *Voyage en Suisse*,

[1] Paul Hugounet, *Mimes et Pierrots* (Paris, 1889), p. 202.

revolved around the vicissitudes of coach and railway travel, and gave full scope to the demoniac physical virtuosity of the Hanlons. These extraordinary Irishmen continued many of the same essentially sad themes with which Debureau had made himself the idol of the French popular theatre in the thirties. The Hanlons, however, in addition to their whimsy were capable of almost frightening effects. Their chief specialty was a weird pantomime consisting of violent struggles not only with each other but also with the furniture, the properties, and indeed anything on the stage. Meticulously dressed for the fracas in camouflaged protective costumes, utilizing their acrobatic skill to make the most comically alarming entries and exits, preparing all their properties to give the maximum impression of violent shattering, enhancing their effects by ferocious grimaces and terrifying exclamations, they executed with rigorous precision a grotesque mixture of acrobatics, ballet, and pantomime. Their productions required infinite finesse of execution and possessed some of the British dramatic quality. Banville describes an interesting feature of their technique in these words:

Suddenly, in a twinkling, with a quick, clever gesture, they indicate what they are going to do, because a real artist scorns mere surprise as a method of amazing us, and feels that he must astonish the spectator even after having put him on the alert ... after having roused his critical faculty. Then having announced the manœuvre they proceed with impeccable perfection, and each evolution gives rise to another development which continues from it.[2]

Their repertoire included several pantomimes in which the broadest comic effects were mingled with the macabre and the violent and which were carried out with the same meticulously timed execution. With these performances the Hanlons seemed to have reached the utmost heights of their peculiar art. Then, as regularly occurs in such cases, the extraordinary vogue which they had created passed very quickly. Their *Voyage en Suisse* began at the Théâtre des Variétés on September 1, 1879, and ran for almost a hundred nights; then the troupe departed for lengthy and profitable tours through Europe and the United States.

Agoust remained after the departure of the Hanlons. He mounted a pantomime vaudeville written for him by a Scotsman, Joseph Mackay, and translated into French under the title *Le Testament de MacFarlane*. This he presented with a mixed English and French troupe at the Comédie Parisienne in October 1881. The star of the production proved to be an Englishman, Fred Desmond, who played the role of a groom with

[2] Cited by Michael Sangor in *La Plume*, September 15, 1892.

exemplary British phlegm, winning from the French critics the odd but flattering tribute of a comparison with Debureau. But the production had what the French termed a "succès contesté," and reached its fiftieth night with some difficulty. When the Hanlon-Lee troupe, not greatly changed in personnel, returned to the Théâtre des Variétés in 1885 to present *Le Naufrage de M. Godat* (by the same author as *Le Voyage en Suisse*), their success was in no way comparable to that enjoyed in 1879. The popularity of this type of entertainment was evidently swiftly disappearing; even those who imitated the Hanlons' violent style did so with such pronounced variations as to bring the productions back into the regular clown traditions.

What was the attraction possessed by these extraordinary artists which appeared peculiarly British in French eyes? Most notable seemed to be the petulant, exasperated violence of their acts. Referring to their violent comedy burlesque, Michael Sangor, writing in *La Plume* in 1892, described them with accuracy from the French point of view as "those strange giddy representatives of English miming," and also, pertinently, styled them as "the last representatives of English agitation, of epilepsy in the pantomime." Their art was, in fact, too strained, too feverish either to enjoy long favour in France or to exert any really profound influence although we find Strehly affirming in 1903: "Since *Le Voyage en Suisse*, English pantomime has taken permanent residence on the boards of our popular theatres. Many a mediocre vaudeville turn, many a play owes a large part of its success to a pantomimed scene."[3]

Paralleling the Hanlons both in time and in technique were a number of individual performers who, like them, stressed pantomime and the grotesque in their acrobatic performances. Most representative of these was Joe Bibb. "A very clever grotesque and clown,"[4] as Thomas Frost describes him, he first appeared in Paris during the 1872-3 season and won immediate popularity. Bibb displayed remarkable versatility, drawing his inspiration from a variety of sources. This is well illustrated by Dalsème's comment on "the original and highly personal waggeries of Bibb as he cunningly plays his role of bumpkin."[5] Bibb, he maintained, was the model of the British comedian with his pretended stupidity and his skilfully contrived mishaps. The critic

---
[3] G. Strehly, *L'Acrobatie et les Acrobates* (Paris, 1903), p. 344.
[4] Thomas Frost, *Circus Life and Circus Celebrities* (London, 1875), p. 306.
[5] A. J. Dalsème, *Le Cirque à pied et à cheval* (Paris, 1888), pp. 168-9.

particularly admired the mixture of pantomime and comical gymnastics which Bibb used, and described his poker-faced pranks as being really "theatre in action." The career of this artist continued through the seventies and was further prolonged by a large number of followers and imitators. But, whatever may have been the case in the theatres, the circus performers, even while the Hanlons and their imitators were enjoying their chief successes, were developing other types of clowns to replace them.

The first of these was the vocal humorist, the *clown parleur*. For, paradoxical as it may appear, it was the English clowns who introduced speech into clowning in the French circuses. Boldly capitalizing on the language difficulty, the British comedians of the seventies and eighties began to talk quite freely, resuming the method which Billy Saunders, the first clown in France, had used. The man who was chiefly responsible for this played as Tony Greace or Grice and, like Kemp twenty-five years before him, made important changes in technique. He resembled the majority of innovators in that he worked with familiar materials but replaced outworn elements with new ones more suited to his powers.[6]

A man of huge proportions, he naturally did not excel as an acrobat; happily for him, the popularity of that type waned during the seventies. He by no means neglected the physically comical; as leading clown in the Nouveau Cirque, he followed the tradition of Richard Baxter by giving caricatures of the ballet dancers' less graceful postures, a parody which his extremely ample bulk made grotesquely comical. He also carried on the tradition of the *clown dresseur*, that is, he presented trained animals (especially a pig, Charlie) which he put through a variety of tricks.

Greace's chief innovation was his development of a clown technique separate from acrobatics. He was frequently a lone performer, carrying on conversations with his trained animals or, more often, entering into dialogues with the audience. This device formed his second innovation. His French was, of course, atrocious, both naturally and intentionally. But the crowds loved the linguistic somersaults of

---

[6] The name of this artist, like those of Phillips, the pantomime dancer of 1737, Bates, the equestrian of 1778, and Penley, the unfortunate impresario of 1822, was probably maltreated in both oral and written form by the French. The Greace version perhaps represented an attempt at a French phonetic rendering of Grace, while the Grice form may have been an heroic endeavour to deal with a Cockney handling of it. The real name seems to have been irretrievably lost.

the English clowns as much as their physical gymnastics. By utilizing language and by performing with lesser clowns, Greace developed the comic sketch as part of the clown's material. In his famous *Chef de Gare* scene his concern for the travellers' welfare varied according to their nationality. The Englishman was solicitously shepherded to a seat and given his luggage; the Italian was shown a vacant compartment; while the Negro was hoisted and kicked in the direction of the third class. The proof of Greace's importance in the field of clowning lies in the number of those who emulated him as pupils, rivals, and unconscious imitators. His long career may be said to have extended itself in the performances of his successors.

Chief among Greace's rivals in his invention of new turns, Billy Hayden represented the *clown parleur* at his highest level. Hayden played in various parts of Europe, at first as a black-face minstrel, and finally discovered his powers as a clown while in Germany. He virtually discarded acrobatics in his performances, his character, according to Perrodil, being "too British for him to forget his original gravity even when acting as a clown."[7] This prince of clowns was a constant parodist. His costume of loose jacket and voluminous trousers of white bore the word *Confiture* across the back in mockery of the clowns who had their names embroidered on their blouses; his shoes were over two feet long, and his make-up made his face a mirth-provoking sight even in repose; his studiously cultivated English accent enhanced all his comic patter. The appearance in the ring of this fantastic figure with his jaunty "Voala, Voala Bonnsoar! Commoncava?" regularly sent the crowd into gales of laughter. "The outlandish jargon," wrote a contemporary, "rarely misses its effect. What a treat to hear a language maltreated!"[8] Hayden is even credited with carrying his bilingual clowning into print. His humour is well illustrated by a fragment from the "Preface" to his supposed treatise on animal training.

Dans oune siecle hou en meme temps qu'aux spiritual faculties, oune si great importance est accodee aux exercisses de la dgymnastique je prends la liberty d'attire l'attenchion de Votre Lordship sour le travail de mes anes boxeurs et de mes couchons sauteurs.[9]

[7] E. de Perrodil, *Monseiur Clown* (Paris, 1889), p. 50.
[8] Dalsème, *Le Cirque à pied et à cheval*, p. 71.
[9] Cited by Dalsème, *ibid.*, p. 73.

Like Greace, Hayden used trained animals and even puppets with which he conversed or to which he related his droll stories. He was remarkably inventive in formulating new acts. One of his novelties was to go into the audience, there to carry on absurd three-cornered wrangles with a confederate in the ring and his supposed friend in the stands, the hapless person beside whom he had sat down. Another of his inventions, still commonly seen in circuses, was to enter in feminine attire with a monumental bustle. The bustle, suddenly left behind by Billy, not only remained upright, but also after a few moments of hilarious indecision, briskly followed and overtook him. Like most geniuses, Hayden was inimitable; his best procedures fell lamentably flat when attempted by imitators. Hayden enjoyed a long and successful career in the Cirque d'Hiver and the Cirque d'Eté. He was recognized not only by the crowds but also by the critics as being a consummate artist. Perrodil says of him, "Billy Hayden ... will remain the model of the talking clown...." And Leroux pays him the high compliment of a comparison with Debureau.

The second of the new types, the *auguste*, was that extraordinary being whom the English generally included with the clowns in spite of his distinctive costume, character, and activities. The *auguste* was the officious busy-body in an over-sized swallow-tail coat, white waistcoat, trousers of varying lengths and widths, white spats, and enormous shoes, who rushed about the ring getting in everyone's way, misdirecting anyone who would listen to his earnest advice, and making a general nuisance of himself. "We know this character's role," wrote Perrodil, "it is to appear enormously busy while doing nothing or even interfering, if he feels like it, with the work of the stage hands."[10] The *auguste* made immense pretensions to gentility; his disdain of what displeased him assumed overwhelming proportions; his patronizing affability and punctilious politeness towards those favoured with his approval marked him as an individual of tremendous importance in his own eyes. Like all the other members of the clown family, this fly-on-the-coach was a parody and his role caricatured the activities of that tyrant of the circus, the ring-master.

The origin of the *auguste* cannot be traced with exactness, but the honour of his creation, development, and finally introduction into France indisputably belongs to three Englishmen: Belling, Chadwick,

[10]Perrodil, *Monseiur Clown*, p. 69.

and Guyon. Belling undoubtedly originated the type. The precise date and circumstances of the *auguste*'s birth are disputed, but according to the most credible version, Belling, an equestrian and occasional comedian, appearing one evening on the stage of a German circus to place a piece of equipment, tripped over a guy-rope and sprawled headlong to the delight of the crowd. Belling's all-too-celebrated alcoholic tendencies added a further touch of humour to the scene. The chorus of *Auguste dumm!* apparently remained in Belling's mind, for he began to develop the comic personage thus suggested, accentuating the elements that proved effective and discarding the unsuccessful ones. Yet it was over a decade later that Belling, making his début at Franconi's in 1877, first billed himself under the pseudonym of *auguste*. Even yet the character was far from established, and Belling frequently appeared as an ordinary clown.

Chadwick, in addition to the secondary clown parts, which have been described above, also played as an *auguste* and contributed a number of items to his character. Indeed, claims are made that even before Belling appeared Chadwick had already given the French a taste of the character. However, at the period of the *auguste*'s greatest popularity, Chadwick was occupied with his responsibilities as ring-master of the Nouveau Cirque.

Jimmy Guyon, who really discovered himself as an *auguste*, played in the great Paris circuses as "Gugusse." Discussing the rival claims in the development of the *auguste*, Perrodil says of Guyon: "It is certain in any case that he popularized the role even though the other [Belling] may have been the unconscious creator."[11] Although he did not depend on gymnastics for his chief appeal, Guyon could perform as a very clever acrobat. One of his favourite turns as the officious ring-master was to become entangled in the trapeze safety-nets as they were being cleared away, be hoisted to a considerable height, and then tumble down them in a series of comical falls to the ground. He also attained considerable celebrity by his grotesque grimaces in which his unusually large lower lip was invaluable. Guyon was first engaged at the Hippodrome de l'Alma when it was opened, and raised the *auguste* to an institution as he delighted the crowds at that immense establishment. The appearance of his solitary figure in tail-coat staggering up the centre of the arena regularly brought forth bursts of applause which

[11]*Ibid.*, p. 75.

continued as he proceeded with his act. He dealt with the vast audience on the personal basis which characterized the *auguste*, with jocularity, confidential intimacy, suspicion, irony, and contempt, all created in his pantomime. Guyon did not completely limit himself to solitary performances. In a sense he foreshadowed the third great innovation of this period by joining Loyal in the presentation of extremely amusing two-character pantomimes. His ten-year career finally came to an end owing to his unfortunate intemperance. Later, his culminating exploit—escaping from the British hospital in Paris in order to see the great clown team of Footitt and Chocolat brought his death from heart failure.

Two other British clowns come into the general *auguste* category, but each had a distinctive attribute. The first, William Bridge, developed as his specialty the aristocratic, distinguished *auguste*, the serious gentleman. Ridiculously enveloped in his impeccable but voluminous garments, lost in his tremendous collar points, shocked and amazed at the misfortunes which assailed him as an innocent bystander in the ring, he rigorously maintained a respectable dignity, belied only by his dishevelled red wig. Bridge was the obvious caricature not only of the ring-master or stage-manager, but also of the serious bourgeois type, with its ideals, aspirations, and discomfitures. He pleased the crowds because of this addition of a recognizable type to the repertoire of the *auguste*.

The third change in the clown figure was produced, as is often the case with humour, by a complete reversal. The last of the individual comedians with whom we deal belongs to a group which the French call *excentriques*, and these they unequivocally describe as being of British origin. Though derived from the *augustes*, who had tended to become solitary performers, the eccentric was squarely opposed to them in nature. The *auguste* was basically a silly, useless, importunate interferer, who caused grief chiefly to himself and who could be considered essentially guileless. The *excentrique*, on the other hand, was an intelligent and self-sufficient, indeed a suspicious individual, solitary by nature. Naturally, the eccentric had no traditions, belonged to no school, followed no pattern; he was simply his peculiar exaggerated self.

The Englishman who began these characters in France, Harry Rolph by name, played under the pseudonym of Little Tich (from Tichborne, where he had performed early in his career). The prefix of Little, a common sobriquet among English comedians, was one of Rolph's contributions to French entertainment circles; Little Tich, however, really lived up, or rather down, to his name as he was only four feet high. He made his début at the Folies Bergères in the early eighties, wearing the oversized *auguste* costume, with the addition of a pair of gargantuan shoes, the length of which was further accentuated by his lack of stature. His specialty was a species of whimsical melancholy, and in this he really instituted a whole school of varied figures. The most brilliant and famous of these was undoubtedly the early Charlie Chaplin, who in costume and technique certainly continued the tradition of Rolph. A second and almost equally famous imitator was the popular French entertainer, Maurice Chevalier. During the first years of the twentieth century Chevalier appeared in a variety of acts, chiefly in cafés, while still in his early teens. His first real triumph came at the age of nineteen at the Eldorado Theatre. For some years the astute and ambitious young artist had been studying the performances of visiting English entertainers. Their grace and agility as dancers particularly impressed him, and his instantaneous popularity at the Eldorado was won, apparently, by an eccentric dance routine based on his observations and recollections of Little Tich.

Little Tich regularly put into caricature a middle-class type, similar to Bridge's gentleman in costume and bearing. His parodies, invariably in the best burlesque style, included most ferocious outbursts of rage from which he would recover abruptly to compose himself with ironic British reserve. All these moods were effected in subtle pantomime. Like so many other British comedians, he also excelled in burlesquing feminine characters. His contrast between the haughty dignity displayed by the débutante with her sweeping train, and the salty language released when she somersaulted backwards over the train, long convulsed Paris audiences. For twenty years he made use of the feminine disguise, another most brilliant and hilarious one being an inevitable parody of Loie Fuller, the American dancer whose graceful veil dances created a considerable stir in Europe, particularly in Paris, around 1890.[12]

Rash critics described this remarkable performer as a genius in his field. While this is too high a claim, he may still be considered a man

[12] Max Nansouty, *Les Trucs au théâtre* (Paris, 1909), *passim*.

of highly original talent. The closing episode of his French career is ironic. After the war of 1914–18 Rolph was recalled from retirement in England to appear once more in Paris, and then this inventive artist, who had originated the style which Chaplin brought to such brilliance, was accused of imitating that actor. Justly incensed, he withdrew from France completely. Though such a figure could never have true followers, there were many who, in one way or another, imitated his oddities, and added their own tricks of speech, scenes, or properties.

The rise of the *auguste* during the seventies and eighties created a problem for his elder brother, the clown. What should be the attitude of the established comedian towards this intruder? The clown could choose among three courses. He could neglect the newcomer, he could oppose him, or he could gain his co-operation in developing new comic techniques. In varying degree, all the important clowns followed one of these courses. No real debate arose over the status of the two figures; the clown remained indisputably on a higher plane in the artists' hierarchy. "Never forget yourself to the point of calling a clown an *auguste* in his presence," Perrodil warns us, "but on the contrary you may call an *auguste* a clown. He will be flattered; he will hold out his hand as a sign of gratitude."[13]

Obviously, the initiative in establishing an act combining the two characters would have to be taken by the clown; thus, if there were to be any co-operation, an individual clown would have to invent an act requiring the special offices of an *auguste*, find a prospective partner, and win his loyalty. For some time this alliance was not very frequent. The clown is an interesting study as an artist who performs in a limited field, but who, to maintain his popularity, must constantly produce the impression of novelty. To this must be added the fact that, despite his feverish search for novelty, the clown is conservative by nature. He cannot afford to risk failure by any ill-conceived venture. He will, consequently, risk undue repetition rather than unsuccessful innovation. It is not, therefore, greatly surprising to find that the leading clowns of the eighties did not incorporate the *auguste* into their acts. What help they required they drew from their puppets, their animals, their audience, or from purely incidental helpers.

The clown who joined forces with an *auguste* in a permanent alliance again came from England. George Footitt grew up with the circus,

[13]Perrodil, *Monsieur Clown*, p. 71.

his father playing as a chief clown. From the age of three the boy appeared in various acts as a miniature edition of Footitt senior. His father's death and his mother's re-marriage placed young George under the direction of his step-father who introduced him to his own art, that of the equestrian. Thus, when Footitt began an independent circus career in 1876, it was as an equestrian acrobat. This strenuous calling he followed for six years before he finally changed to clowning. The reasons remain vague; whether it was, as he maintained, from having lost his horse at gambling, or because of the possibility of concealing his unprepossessing face, or the realization that the career of clown was likely to be less strenuous and hence much longer than that of equestrian, Footitt made the change.

He was not entering an uncontested field. In 1885, Billy Hayden, Greace, the Spanish clown Medrano, not to mention Guyon, all were high in popular favour, while below them a host of lesser clowns frantically endeavoured to rise above the crowd. From the beginning Footitt had two advantages. His equestrian skill enabled him to present uproariously funny parodies of the equestrian stars. An early appearance at Covent Garden with the Great International Circus was in his parody, *L'Ecuyère au panneau*, and in this, with whitened clown's face and that favourite costume of so many English comedians, feminine attire (on this occasion it was the gauze skirt of the equestrienne), he brought down the house. During the following years Footitt alternated between England and France. In Paris in 1890, playing in rivalry with Hayden at Franconi's and also in the clown troupe of Greace at the Nouveau Cirque, he finally achieved the position of leading comedian.

Up to that point Footitt had shown himself to be simply a very good clown with an equestrian side-line. His phenomenal success was attained with the aid of the new circus figure, the *auguste*. Neither the origins nor the real name of his partner Chocolat have ever been discovered although he seems to have come from the West Indies. Recognized as a natural *auguste* by Greace who encountered him in Spain, Chocolat entered that famous clown's employ and remained with the Nouveau Cirque in various passive roles for Greace and the troupe in general. Awkward, guileless, ignorant, Chocolat seemed designed to be the butt of all the practical jokes, temperamental outbursts, thrashings, and indignities in every presentation. For example, he regularly played the part of the luckless third class passenger in Greace's *Chef de Gare*. The combination of the imperturbable Chocolat and the violently impatient Footitt was obviously marked for success. The association between clown and *auguste* became permanent and they finally formed an inseparable unit in the minds of the public.

The ideas for their performances came from Footitt, who possessed that almost painful sensitivity to life which marks the true artist. As a result of this, the sketches regularly took their departure in the real and made a flight into the hyperbolical and preposterous, the combination implicit in much humorous writing. As well, with the cautious inventiveness of the true clown, Footitt restored to the circus the comical interludes in dialogue form which had largely disappeared with the pantomime.

It was, indeed, principally in these comical two-person sketches that the partners attracted the public. Particularly gifted in displaying the emotions of fear and rage, accentuating his authoritarian, testy character, Footitt frothed endlessly around the unshakeably tranquil stupidity of Chocolat, a tranquillity which at times vanquished the frenzied tantrums of his tormentor. Footitt was, of course, enough of an artist to realize that all the punishment must not go in the same direction. In the lusty give and take of clowning, it was inevitable that he himself would occasionally be exceedingly discomfited. Consequently, from time to time, in order to give variety to their act the clown would momentarily assume the *auguste*'s role of butt and victim. In general, however, Footitt's tyrannical domineering was plain even to the placidly obtuse Chocolat. The two provided perfect foils for each other: Footitt personifying the eternally dissatisfied, pouting, exasperated type, his drawn-down mouth accentuated by his lurid make-up, and Chocolat typifying resignation and patient stolidity.

In his early success, *L'Ecuyère au panneau*, Footitt had appeared in woman's clothes, as we have seen, and this typical English comedian continued to be representative in this type of role also; for thirty years he ran the gamut of ridiculous female impersonations, from cooks to queens. The triumphal appearance of Sarah Bernhardt in Sardou's *Cléopâtre* occasioned his most sensational feminine role. Footitt's version, complete with a tousled red wig à la Bernhardt and a rubber serpent, which, after biting the queen, bowed to the audience before retiring, improved on the original by including a resurrection. In this startling sequel, the defunct queen leapt abruptly to her feet, rushed desperately around the ring, her train slung over her arm and Chocolat in frantic pursuit, bounded onto a strategically placed spring-board and, after a triple aerial somersault, disappeared down an exit tunnel. Indirect representations from the great actress brought promises of withdrawal, which Footitt regularly failed to keep. Even Mlle Bernhardt's personal appearance at a performance did not deter him. The illustrious victim managed to retain an icy *hauteur* through the body of the act, but was unable to withstand the wonderful last scene and joined in the universal hilarity.[14]

The popularity of Footitt and Chocolat in the nineties was largely due to their partnership. Although Footitt continued to appear in the twentieth century, his significance from our point of view ends with his years opposite Chocolat at the Nouveau Cirque. As well as being the greatest of British clowns in France in ability and prestige, he was the last British comic to exert influence. There is no question regarding his stature as a comic entertainer and his popularity on all levels in France. He was not merely admired and applauded by the crowds; he also became a legendary figure among journalists, men of letters, and even artists. Like many such figures, he marked the end of an era.

As with Shakespearean drama, so with the clown, certain elements proved so foreign as to be quite unacceptable to the French. Discussing the hyperbolic, grotesque and even macabre clowning apparently relished by the English, Henri Frichet pertinently comments: "Their gaiety is not the same as ours, and the psychology of their laughter often eludes us."[15] The prestige of a brilliant performer such as Kemble, Macready, Boswell, or Footitt might result in temporary sufferance of these elements but it could not ensure permanent acceptance of them. The refusal of the French to accept such foreign elements as the ferocity of the Hanlon pantomimes simply marked the extent to which the English clown could influence the French. M. Rémy phrases this point well: "The fantastic, artificial, and voluntarily exaggerated tendencies of English pantomimists clashed with Parisian customs and tastes. It was, on the contrary, by emphasizing the witty, let us say human,

[14]Gabriel Astruc, *Le Pavillon des fantômes* (Paris, 1929), *passim*.
[15]Henri Frichet, *Le Cirque et les forains* (Paris, 1898), p. 71.

elements of farce and buffooning that the English clown was able to achieve success on our stages."[16]

In this avowedly unilateral examination, the clowns of other nations have been almost entirely neglected. But there were many of them in Paris, and when the whimsical or macabre elements of British clowning became too marked some other foreign visitor supplied what was more acceptable. Medrano, the Spanish clown and director, for example, at the close of the century capitalized on what he advertised as a *théâtre gai*, obviously presented as an antidote to the splenetic *clown britannique*. His notable success is an apt illustration of the counterbalance provided by non-British entertainers for the peculiar qualities of the British clowns.

[16] Tristan Rémy, *Les Clowns* (Paris, 1945), p. 88.

14 · The Why and Wherefore

The story of British entertainers in France does not conclude with the visit of Charles James Mathews or with the careers of Footitt and Chocolat, but it seems judicious for various reasons to conclude this account with those performances.

Individual visits across the Channel continued throughout the nineteenth century. John Kemble not only spent several years as a student in the English college at Douai, but also visited Paris on several occasions, notably in 1802 during the Peace of Amiens. There he associated with Talma and other members of the Comédie Française. Indeed, Kemble retired to Toulouse for the last years of his life. A great admirer of French actors and their theatre, he borrowed from them many ideas regarding costumes, scenery, and interpretation, in all of which he instituted progressive reforms in his London company. His brother, Charles Kemble, appeared in Brussels and Boulogne before occupation officers and dignitaries shortly after Waterloo. He also visited Paris, but no record remains that he played there before 1827.

The London actress and dramatic teacher, Fanny Kelly, forged another link with France. Fired with ambition to go on the stage, she was hurried off to Paris by her parents to dissuade her from the idea. The opposite effect was attained; inspired by the drama which she saw in the French capital, Miss Kelly determined to embrace a stage career. This decision was certainly influenced by her recitations of Shakespeare before Talma.

The actor Morris Barnett, though not in the same rank as Kean or Macready, held an honourable place on the London stage in the eighteen-forties. Barnett spent the early part of his life in France, and his outstanding capacity in portraying French characters certainly came from first-hand observation and experience. In 1845 we find a Miss Isabella Glen also in Paris engaged in dramatic studies. Her training was clearly reflected in the declamatory style of her later appearances in England when she returned in 1846, apparently never to visit France again.

A more notable student appeared some thirty years later in the person of Miss Genevieve Ward, who in 1877 went to Paris to study under Régnier. She made her début as Lady Macbeth, playing in French. The *Revue britannique* of February, 1877, reported: "In the sleepwalking scene ... she was positively admirable. Never have remorse or the terrors of hallucination been so poignantly interpreted; the whole theatre hung on her lips and shuddered with her." Miss Ward received the signal honour of an invitation to join the troupe of the Théâtre Français. Unfortunately, as a result of the opposition of a leading *sociétaire*, she was prevented from playing there. In London Miss Ward frequently played in French as well as English.[1]

There were further appearances of English-speaking (though not British) troupes in the nineteenth century. The American actor, J. Austen Daly, headed a touring company which he took to Berlin and Paris in 1886. Though he did not receive an enthusiastic reception, he returned two years later. His second production, Shakespeare's *The Taming of the Shrew*, still received only mild acclaim. In 1891 Mr. Daly again appeared in Paris with a double bill, *As You Like It* and *The School for Scandal*, both of which roused considerably more cordial comment than the earlier offerings.

Although the theatrical visits of the twentieth century are beyond our limits, a few of the most important may be noted. In 1911 Mr. George Edward brought *The Quaker Girl* to Paris for a brief run. Between the wars Sir Alfred Butt made an unsuccessful experiment with a mixed English-French company. We also note the presentation of *Candida* in 1939 with Diana Wynyard in the leading role, and the popular visit of the Old Vic company after the Second World War.

In pantomime English visits continued at extended intervals. Towards the close of the century the Lauri family, billed as the Lauri-Lauris, appeared at the Châtelet and other *théâtres à grand spectacle* in a number of pantomimes which mildly recalled the frenzied productions of the Hanlon-Lees. *The Terrible Night*, *Maison tranquille*, and the animated *Puss Puss* left somewhat the same impression in Parisian minds as did *Le Voyage en Suisse*. In 1908 the pantomime *Peter Pan* came to the Vaudeville theatre with Pauline Chase as Peter and Miss Hilda Trevelyan (half French by birth) as Wendy. Cordially received by the critics and the public, the production even raised the question of arranging a French version.

[1]Dame Genevieve Ward, *Before and Behind the Curtain* (London, 1918), *passim*.

Memories of the energetic amateur efforts of the officers in 1815 are inevitably recalled by the many troupes which appeared behind the British lines in 1917 and 1918. M. Emile Henriot in *L'Illustration* of November, 1918, comments on the elaborate organization and polished performance of such a company. These players he encountered in Valenciennes, the scene of similar activities almost exactly a century before. An interesting contrast is apparent between the two groups of entertainers. After Waterloo a group of officers engaged in literary theatrical productions for the pleasure of their fellow officers; in 1918 the entertainment was provided by men recruited from all ranks and entry into the company depended upon the individual's qualifications as a performer. The audiences of 1816, composed of aristocratic groups enjoying peace-time garrison life, were replaced in 1918 by battalions of weary troops snatching momentary respite from active warfare.

The point to be made with regard to each of these briefly mentioned appearances is precisely the one just stressed in connection with amateur army theatricals; they had been done before. By the close of the nineteenth century, all the basic elements of English visits to France had repeatedly appeared. Indeed it might be said that the three chief types of performers, actors, clowns, and equestrians, all appeared within less than thirty years of the very beginning of the visits. In 1583 English acrobats or clowns visited Paris, in 1604 Shakespearean actors entertained the French court, and in 1608 Mr. Banks displayed his trained horse in pantomime performances. In a broad sense British performers in France have simply repeated, with immense variations and elaborations, these three types of entertainment.

The complete success of any visit required the simultaneous existence of two elements: a favourable political climate and a theatrical situation favourable to the visitors. These two factors did not invariably coincide. The English dancers who, in 1671, received permission to appear in Paris were granted entry by no less a person than Louis XIV, who felt kindly disposed towards England.[2] That country had recently restored his *protégés*, the Stuarts, and signed the Treaty of Dover. However, competition must have been too keen for the troupe since no record remains of their performances. Then, in the seventeen-fifties,

[2] Among the French court documents of 1671 is to be found an order from Louis granting permission to a troupe of English dancers to give performances for three months in the capital from the end of March forward. Whether these artists availed themselves of their privilege is not known, since no mention of them occurs elsewhere. See F. W. Lindsay, *Dramatic Parody by Marionettes in 18th Century Paris* (New York, 1946), p. 15.

when local difficulties were throttling the Opéra Comique, and when Monnet showed himself ready to bring in artists from abroad, jingoistic sentiment on both sides of the Channel made artistic exchange almost impossible. An interesting deviation from the general rule (if the reasons given were genuine) appeared at this time in the rebuff of a group of British performers seeking to present *The Beggar's Opera* in Paris. The refusal was based not on the grounds of nationality, but on the argument that their version was unsatisfactory artistically.[3]

An example of an unhappy lack of coincidence in artistic and political climates occurred in the early eighteen-twenties. After the death of Napoleon, chauvinism fermented dangerously despite the cosmopolitan attitude of the Romantics. French popular plays lampooned the English as raucously as the censorship would permit. A typical instance of the absurd extremes to which matters went may be seen in a brief theatrical incident. The French actor who played the role of Hudson Lowe (Napoleon's English military jailer) in a popular play about the dead emperor, moved in virtual fear of his life. On one occasion, having been recognized and treed by a mob of rabid Anglophobes, the unfortunate artist was rescued and escorted home only by strong police action. While visiting artists would not take the political barometer as the final arbiter, it is still probable that their successes in France, in so far as they were affected by the political climate, would certainly encourage or deter other troupes. The Penley season is a case in point.

These remarks may appear extreme, but it should be remembered that the attitudes of audiences were frequently marked by violence during the Romantic period in France. The French took their theatre seriously. The brutality which met Penley's company was matched, indeed considerably exceeded, by the furores raised over completely French plays not only in Paris but also in the provinces. The *parterre*, the terror of French dramatists and directors, frequently became a rallying point for the brasher and more rowdy theatrical devotees. These individuals, with all the fervour and roughly the intelligence of Hyde Park hecklers, occasionally made it impossible for foreign artists to proceed.

The reasons for the chief visits by British performers are interesting. Only rarely were these journeys escapes from unfavourable conditions

[3] F. C. Green, *Minuet* (London, 1935), p. 18.

at home; rather, they took place because of favourable conditions in France. Even the days of the Puritan Commonwealth in England did not see a single attempt by harassed artists to seek better luck across the Channel. Indeed, it can fairly be argued that, on the contrary, it was when the English theatre was flourishing and popular that any exodus took place. In periods of lively demand, more and more persons began acting and surpluses inevitably arose. A certain proportion of these would naturally be tempted to seek fortune away from keen competition at home. Such cases are to be seen in 1604, the hey-day of Elizabethan drama; in the seventeen-thirties and forties, when English pantomime reigned supreme; and in 1827, when a whole group of giants, both veteran and youthful, crowded the London stage. It was not always the best who visited Paris, but rather all categories with many different reasons. Such first rank artists as Kean, Kemble, Macready, Miss Foote, and Helena Faucit simply sought fresh fields to conquer. But such earnest utility performers as Penley, Abbot, and the Wallacks, or an actress such as Harriet Smithson, strangely rejected in England, were obviously seeking any field in which to display what talents they possessed.

The word favourable, used in connection with the situation in France, requires clarification. Frequently what the English artists considered favourable circumstances were the reverse from the viewpoint of the ordinary French theatre-goer. Certainly several of the most successful British visits were at periods when native competition was low. In 1604, for example, the French theatre remained largely under an academic monopoly; Alexandre Hardy's popular productions were yet to come. In the seventeen-thirties the French pantomime still lacked a great Harlequin figure to replace the Englishman Baxter; the Italian vein of inspiration had run very thin, and no outstanding native figure had arisen. Little surprise is aroused at the striking triumphs of the British dancers and pantomime actors who dominated the stages of the fairs at that time. The eighteen-twenties were marked by widespread and vociferous dissatisfaction among Parisian theatre patrons. Their theatrical fare was regularly composed either of bad imitations of the classics or worse adaptations of foreign plays. When indifferent interpretation was added to dubious material, it is easy to see that any fresh element would be welcome. Thus, a theatrical situation unfavourable to the public could be regarded as favourable to the cross-Channel visitors.

However, eager as they may have been to view and enjoy novel artistic productions, the French very rarely consented to accept them outright. Rather, they maintained with tenacity both their critical faculty and their right of choice. The modifications and adaptations which occur when one nation borrows from the literature of another form a great part of the charm of the study of comparative literature. So, in the matter of dramatic incursions from England into France, there is much to interest us in the distinctively French receptions accorded to both the human and the literary importations.

Cordial as the French critics were, in general, they applied their critical tenets with conscientious rigour. Their judicial attitude was largely reflected by the public as well as by those playwrights who imitated the foreign works and those actors who chose to imitate their visiting *confrères*. The imitations and adaptations were particularly marked among the performers of the eighteenth century, that is, the pantomimists or equestrians. Here the imitation was most frequently in the field of physical techniques, such as dance steps or equestrian feats. It is interesting to notice that in many cases the imitation was either immediately or ultimately so modified that it lost almost all traces of its foreign origin and became virtually French. This is partly explained by the natural tendency of the French imitators to select only those features which appealed to them and for which they would probably have some innate aptitude.

In the nineteenth century many French actors watched and copied the playing of the British troupes. The enthusiastic and extreme tendencies of the French Romantic period carried some of the younger artists to regrettable and ridiculous lengths in the eighteen-thirties, as the theatrical journals of the time make very clear. English vigour in the pantomime proved a revelation to the French and left marked traces on Parisian technique. Most impressive of all the foreign elements to the Parisians was the intensely dramatic quality of all the British productions, whether in theatre, pantomime, equestrian displays, or clowning. There seems little doubt that whatever success the theatrical invaders enjoyed arose chiefly from this inherently dramatic character in their material, as well as in the interpretation. The vitality of Shakespeare's plays, which enabled them to survive even the massacring to which they were subjected in the early nineteenth century, won keen appreciation when they were presented in less mangled form by the London players. And, in the eyes of the French, the vitality of the playwright was largely matched by the zest of his compatriots as they presented his dramas.

Equally marked was the complete rejection by both critics and public of certain British elements. The very quality of robustness which has just been mentioned led occasionally to extreme forms which Gallic audiences found unacceptable. Gusto they appreciated, sheer violence on the physical plane repelled them. The people who keenly appreciated the tragedies of Racine in which only words cut and slay, were unable to face the physical excesses in *Othello* and *Lear*. The little Dauphin of 1604, with his reaction to a decapitation, was echoed in the criticism directed by Baudelaire against the crude violences of Tom Mathews' pantomime clowns. One of his chief strictures he directed against the regrettable Anglo-Saxon tendency to remove heads. In general, however, in spite of the limitations imposed by *les bienséances*, it was by the portrayal of physical anguish and of death that the visiting actors especially impressed their Parisian audiences.

A common denominator among the many and varied visits is found in the formidable barrier presented by the language problem. This was met in several ways. There were, on the one hand, those who really did not have to cope with the difficulty: the acrobats of the sixteenth century, the learned horse of Mr. Banks in 1608, the pantomime dancers of the eighteenth century, Mr. Astley's four-footed performers and their riders, all evaded the problem by using no language. In a few cases, on the other hand, the English visitors actually spoke French. There is no doubt that Richard Baxter, a long-time resident of France, could handle a French role. One hundred years later, Abbot not only did the honours for his troupe in French, but also performed in French with members of the Comédie Française. Though some of the criticisms levelled at Charles James Mathews in 1865 were sharp enough, there seems little doubt that his French was quite adequate for the appreciation of his role by any French spectator of good will. Among the British clowns who dominated the Parisian scene there were those who, like Billy Hayden, made great capital out of the fantastic jargon which resulted from their cavalier attempts to speak French.

All these cases are, however, of a special nature. The real test was faced by those courageous troupes of the nineteenth century who brought to Paris productions which depended for their true appreciation on an adequate understanding of English. A scrupulous reading of the criticisms rendered by the Parisian judges leaves one convinced that, with the exception of a few Anglophils, such as Charles Nodier, who knew English thoroughly, only a scanty proportion of those who attended really understood the plays. The hostile critics gleefully used this fact to illustrate their moral, the benevolent admitted with regret that much must have escaped them. The correspondent for *Le Réveil* wrote, for example, on August 21, 1822: "We intend to visit the other productions of Mr. Penley; and as it is not unknown in literature to judge what you do not understand, we will attend Mr. Penley's presentation without understanding it, but at least we will listen to it." Similarly in January, 1828, the moderately sympathetic *La Pandore* explained a disappointing attendance at Richard III: "The *dilettanti* are beginning to realize that they do not understand English. M. Laurent would be wise to reduce the number of his English performances or at least to bring some new actors."

Charles Kemble apparently felt that the French audiences of 1827–8 actually understood relatively little of the plays but enjoyed the action and bustle of the stage business. He quotes one enthusiastic Frenchman's opinion on *Othello*, "There is real passion and tragedy for you! How I love that play! There is so much uproar in it."[4] Similar doubt as to comprehension was expressed in 1829 by Emile Deschamps, an ardent supporter of international literary borrowing. In his *Etudes françaises et étrangères* he urged the presentation of Shakespeare in vital translation, with the necessary grandeur of setting and vigour of interpretation. No real conception of Shakespeare, he protested, could be given either by presentations in English where over three-quarters of the spectators could not understand a word, or by dull prose translations. The truth of this contention is borne out by the relative popularity of plays in the repertoires of the visiting companies. Comedies like those of Sheridan, which depended on verbal manœuvrings or brilliance of phrasing, never made much of an impression. It was, on the contrary, the relatively melodramatic productions of

[4] W. J. Lawrence, "English Players in France" in *The Gentleman's Magazine*, May 1890.

Shakespeare and others which really held the boards. *Macbeth, Jane Shore, William Tell*, these plays, with their abundant peripetia, their frequent tableaux, and their numerous opportunities for business and pantomime, were consistently the highlights of the visits.

The most striking feature of the English presentations in French eyes was indubitably the remarkable power of pantomime displayed by the British players. We recall that Garrick had made a profound impression on his French admirers sixty years previously by the mingled vividness and realism of his pantomime. Noverre sums up the matter well in a eulogistic letter written in 1760 before the famous visit to France: "One can without partiality consider him to be the Roscius of England since with fire, diction, delivery, spirit, naturalness, wit, and insight he combines that pantomime ... which marks the great actor and the perfect player."[5] In 1827 the critic of the *Globe* quickly remarked this, writing on October 6, "Their pantomime is at times much nearer to nature than is ours." In the same article Miss Smithson's pantomime is described as admirable. At the close of the long season the critic still remained impressed by the force and beauty of the visitors' mute play. Of Kean, playing the choleric Sir Giles Overeach at the denouement of *A New Way to Pay Old Debts* he wrote, "His surprise, stupor, and despair, his rage, at first strong and later mutely apoplectic are represented with the most frightening reality by Kean." And of his great rival Macready, appearing a month later (July 1828) in *William Tell*, we read: "He begins a succession of scenes which one must have witnessed in order to realize to what heights pantomime can rise and what a host of deep, tender, and powerful emotions Macready is able to express by it." *La Pandore*, frequently less enthusiastic than the Anglophil *Globe* none the less paid frequent tribute to this element of the visitors' art. Of Macready we read in the issue of May 3: "He consistently showed good expression and his pantomime is outstanding." The critic of *L'Incorruptible* on May 30, 1828, expressed his admiration of Kean in these words: "I have never seen anything more heartrending, more genuine, more awful than Kean's grief in these last scenes." Even Abbot rose to the heights on occasion, as is suggested by the following words from the same

---

[5]Cited in Alexandre Ricord (aîné), *Les Fastes de la Comédie Française* (Paris, 1821-2; 2 vols.), I, p. 116.

journal's comment on the same date, "One can glimpse by this brief scene to what an extent the English actors are superior to ours in the expression of grief and pathos."

To comment that the British visitors played their pantomime to the utmost limit is to emphasize the evident. Recognizing the severe limits of verbal comprehension in Paris and their admitted superiority in mute play, the actors naturally mimed as frequently and tellingly as possible. Thus, the basic means of communication constantly remained pantomime in which the British players were, happily, excellent. But it must not be forgotten that the mime artist is universally regarded as the supreme actor, as truly international as any artist can ever be in his appeal.

In other areas the French maintained and repeatedly upheld French superiority as, for example, in settings and costumes. It may be argued that the limited means of the visitors precluded a representative display of English stagecraft. In justice, however, it must be admitted that London had much to learn from Paris in these respects. The visits both of individual artists and of companies from Betterton in 1672 to the various individual and corporate appearances of the nineteenth century had considerable and beneficial effects on English theatre.

A repeated phenomenon in the visits which have been discussed was that imitation of the foreign entertainers and their techniques was usually so vigorous and considerable that late-comers to Paris from the British Isles found themselves being equalled or even excelled in their specialties by native performers. The pantomime dancers who dominated the stage of the fairs found themselves relatively unimportant after the Seven Years' War. The French had even sent their dancers across the Channel to receive the plaudits of London audiences and to garner ideas for subsequent performances at home. The revenge of the French circuses after Astley's domination of the seventeen-eighties has already been noted. In the case of the other great circus figure, that of the clown, the British domination continued; it was not, indeed, until the beginning of the twentieth century that the Continent began to produce clowns who could defy British competition. The famous Swiss clown Grock, an international figure in the twenties, best marks this stage of development.

In the case of imitation on the legitimate stage no complete parallel can be formed since the language of the French imitators was different.

However, there is no doubt that the vigorous interpretations of 1827, 1829, and 1844 left their mark on many Parisian actors. There were adaptations along with occasional exaggerations (as the critics noticed). Indeed, it may well be that this invigoration of the French stage may have had something to do with the long absence of English-speaking presentations in Paris in the last half of the century.

If there is one central thesis to be advanced with regard to the British visitors it is precisely this idea of acceptance, adaptation, and eventual return. When the visitors introduced a new technique or medium, whether pantomime, equestrian performances, a romantic style of acting, or the various clown specialties, the French accepted it after due criticism, revised it to their taste, and then proceeded to develop their own performers. These artists eventually became skilful enough to satisfy the home demand and occasionally even carried some of the original import back to England.

A recent international gesture in Paris may not perhaps provoke a similar one in London; nevertheless it is pleasant to relate it. After the war, in the beautiful Bois de Boulogne park, a formal garden containing a small open-air theatre for the presentation of his plays was dedicated to Shakespeare. Kenneth Mathews described the setting in *The Listener* of July 16, 1953. "The auditorium," he tells us, "is surrounded by raised flower beds growing Shakespearean flowers.... The stage might best be described as a rock garden because there is a small grass plot in front with a towering background of rocks, planted with spires of yew and intersected by winding paths along which the players make their entrances and exits. There is a cave too which turned out to be a most useful piece of stage machinery. There is even a waterfall."

Against this charming background a group of young actors from the Oxford University Dramatic Society gave *Troilus and Cressida* in what we are told were effective and moderately authentic costumes. The distinguished audience was composed of British and French devotees of the theatre with a sprinkling of Americans and a few diplomatic representatives. It is to be hoped that such gracious international contacts may long continue.

Exchange of entertainment is today a common international fact. Artists now cross oceans for even a single performance; radio carries their voices around the world; and they cross international boundaries by means of the motion picture. The study of artistic exchange on the basis of personal appearance has become largely fruitless. We may best conclude by paying a general tribute to those performers who originally ventured abroad to take with them something of British poetry or humour, grace or dexterity. They were not all of equal quality, and only the best could hope to have much effect on France. But, at this distance, we can afford to be charitable towards even the lesser stars and to remember each one as being in his own way a conscious or unwitting artistic ambassador.

Appendix

A TABULAR RECORD OF VISITS TO FRANCE BY BRITISH ARTISTS FROM 1583 TO THE REVOLUTION

1583 English acrobats visit Paris.
1597 English and Spanish acrobats perform in Paris.
1598 Jehan Sehais, *comédien anglais*, presents plays in the Hôtel de Bourgogne during May. Evicted June 4.
1601 Will Kempe, Shakespearean clown and dancer, traverses France *en route* to Italy.
1602 First recorded staging of plays in English; Jesuit colleges at Douai and Saint Omer.
1604 English players present a Shakespearean play at court of Henri IV in September.
1608 Banks exhibits his trained horse Morocco in Paris and Orléans.
1661 Thomas Betterton visits Paris to examine French theatres.
1670 Joe Haynes dances at the première of *Le Bourgeois Gentilhomme* on October 4.
1671 Betterton and Haynes visit Paris to examine the French opera and theatres.
1676 Antoine and François Desvaux, strolling entertainers, visit Dijon.
1678 English dancers appear in *Les Forces de l'amour et de la magie*.
1678 Joseph Clark, posture-maker and contortionist, appears in Paris in the train of the Duke of Buckingham.
1679 Jacques Ozière, marionettist, performs at Dijon.
1679 Woolton brothers set up a circus at Dijon.
1682 Betterton visits Paris to observe the theatres for the king.
1688 Madeleine Rabresel, the Scottish widow of a marionettist, passes through Troyes with her son Gregory.
1707–11 Richard Baxter, pantomime dancer, collaborates with Nivellon at the fairs.
1712–16 Baxter acts as co-manager with Saurin of Madame Baron's pantomime troupe, as well as dancing Harlequin roles.
1713 *Harlequin, invisible chez le Roi de Chine pièce à écriteaux* by Lesage.
1714 *Arlequin Mahomet*, a parodic *opéra comique*, with *vaudevilles*, *Le Tombeau de Nostradamus*, by Lesage.
1715 *Le Temple du Destin*, *opéra comique*, by Lesage, with divertissements.
1716 *Arlequin divin ou Le Lendemain de Noces*, comic opera by Fuzelier. *Harlequin Hubla ou La femme répudiée*, comic opera of Lesage and Dorneval.
1717–18 Baxter and Saurin play in the provinces.
1719–20 *Grande troupe allemande, anglaise et écossaise* presented at Saint Laurent fair by Alard.

1721 Baxter, Saurin, and associates organize an *opéra comique* troupe at Saint Laurent fair. After its failure Baxter retires.
1724 M. Carnivelle, *saltimbanque anglais*, at Saint Germain fair with a small menagerie.
1726 John Rinner erects a *jeu de paume* theatre for his dancers, pantomimists and marionettes.
1727 An outstanding English acrobat appears with Restier's troupe.
1728 Pontou, director of Opéra Comique, brings troupe of English acrobats to perform in the interludes at the fairs.
1729 Dancer Renton carries a special role in *La Noce anglaise* at Saint Laurent fair.
1731 Renton and Haughton join with French mime artist Roger in a divertissement entitled *La Guinguette anglaise* at Saint Laurent fair.
1731 English pantomime troupe appears at Saint Laurent fair, also giving a command performance at Versailles in September.
1737 English dancer Roberts (or Roberti) performs in an interlude of the Opéra Comique presentation at Saint Germain fair.
1737 In June and in August pantomime dancer Phillips gives a variety of pantomime numbers at Saint Germain fair with his wife, daughter and a small company.
1738 Roberts appears at Saint Germain fair in a prologue, *Le Carnaval*.
1738 Henry Delamain, an English pantomime dancer and director, enjoys an outstanding success at the Saint Laurent fair. Roberts dances leading roles along with Torse and La Tour.
1739 Delamain's company plays at both fairs under auspices of Pontou, director of the Opéra Comique. Company disbands at the close of the season.
1740 Roberts dances in the *Grande Troupe Etrangère* along with Hendrick and Ferguson.
1742 English dancer Germain and his sister Frederica take pantomime roles with the *Grande Troupe Etrangère* at Saint Germain fair.
1744 La Pierre, probably of Huguenot origin, carries a pantomime role at Saint Laurent fair.
1745 Mr. Mathews, an English pantomime director, brings a company to the Opéra Comique stage under the auspices of Favart.
1746 Mrs. Sandham presents a company in a complete season at Saint Germain fair.
1746 English female Hercules appears at Saint Germain fair.
1747 English pantomime company brought by directors of the *Opéra Comique Pantomime* and performs throughout Saint Germain season.
1748 English company continues as *Opéra Comique Pantomime*.
1749 *Opéra Comique Pantomime* continues. Bienfait, a marionettist, presents a troupe of Italian and English children in a *pantomime anglaise* at the Saint Germain fair.
1751 Garrick visits Paris in July.
Mrs. Theo. Cibber sent to France by John Rich to recruit dancers for Covent Garden theatre.

1753	*Petits danseurs anglais et hollandais* perform at Saint Germain fair, probably under Bienfait's direction.
1763–5	Garrick pays two extended visits to Paris during his continental tour.
1774	English equestrian Hyam appears at the Colysée with his company. The naturalist Wildman displays his trained bees. Jonas, an English Jew, proves very popular as a juggler and magician at the fairs and in society.
1775	Hyam continues his performances at the Ruggieri Hall and at Armand's Café, Boulevard du Temple, in collaboration with a mechanical display *Les Fêtes de Pluton* directed by an Englishman, Telocin.
1776	Spanish and English dancers and pantomimists appear at Sainte Ovide fair.
1783	Thomas Holcroft spends several months in Paris as correspondent and translator.
1784	Holcroft visits Paris to pirate an acting version of *Le Mariage de Figaro*.
1787	Nicolet presents *La Troupe Royale de Londres* in pantomimes at Saint Germain fair.
1788	*La Troupe Royale de Londres* again appears at Saint Germain fair.
1795	Thomas Holcroft escapes as a political refugee to France, and remains there for several years.

Bibliography

NOTE: This bibliography is selected from a considerably larger body of works touching on the subject, and represents the more pertinent materials which a reader might consult.

BOOKS

Albert, Maurice. *Les Théâtres de la foire*. Paris, 1900.
——— *Les Théâtres des boulevards*. Paris, 1902.
Anonymous (Mlle B^{xxx} née de V^{xxx}). *Le Cirque Olympique*. Paris, 1817.
Archer, William. *William Charles Macready*. London, 1890.
——— *About the Theatre*. London, 1890.
Astruc, Gabriel. *Le Pavillon des fantômes*. Paris, 1929.
Bachaumont Louis Petit de. *Mémoires secrets*, édités par Maisrobert et Mouffle d'Angesville. Paris, 1777 et seq.
Baker, H. Barton. *The London Stage, Its History and Traditions from 1576 to 1888*. 2 vols. London, 1889.
Barberet, V. *Lesage et le théâtre de la foire*. Nancy, 1887.
Baudelaire, Charles. *Oeuvres complètes*. Paris, 1868. Tome 2: "De l'essence du rire et généralement du comique dans les arts plastiques."
Beaulieu, Henri. *Les Théâtres du boulevard du crime. 1752-1862*. Paris, 1905.
Berlioz, Hector. *Mémoires*. Paris, 1870.
——— *Lettres intimes, avec une préface par Charles Gounod*. Paris, 1882.
Bonnet, Jacques. *Histoire générale de la danse sacrée et prophane . . . avec un supplément de la musique, et le parallèle de la peinture et de la poésie* (avec l'Abbé P. Bourdelet). Paris, 1723.
Borgerhoff, J. L. *Le Théâtre anglais à Paris sous la Restauration*. Paris, 1912.
Boudet, Antoine. *Les Affiches de Paris*. 5 vols. Paris, 1746-50.
Bouteiller, J. E. *Histoire complète et méthodique des théâtres de Rouen*. 4 vols. Rouen, 1860-80.
Boysse, E. *Le Théâtre des Jésuites*. Paris, 1880.
Brazier, N. *Histoire des petits théâtres*. Paris, 1839.
Campardon, Emile. *Les Spectacles de la foire*. 2 vols. Paris, 1877.
Capelle, Pierre Adolphe. *Dictionnaire de Morale, de science et de littérature, ou, Choix de pensées ingénieuses et sublimes, de dissertations et de définitions, extraites des plus célèbres moralistes orateurs poètes et savants*. Paris, 1810.
Christian, Arthur. *Etudes sur le Paris d'autrefois*. VIIe série: *Les Jeux équestres*. Paris, 1907.

Collé, C. *Journal et Mémoires*. 3 vols. Paris, 1868.
Collier, J. Payne. *Memoirs of the Principal Actors in the Plays of Shakespeare*. London Shakespeare Society, 1846.
D'Auriac, E. *Le Théâtre de la foire*. Paris, 1878.
Dalsème, A. J. *Le Cirque à pied et à cheval*. Paris, 1888.
Davies, Thomas. *Memoirs of the Life of David Garrick*. London, 1824.
Decastro, J. *The Memoirs of J. D. Comedian*. London, 1824.
Delacroix, Eugène. *Journal d'Eugène Delacroix, édité par André Joubin*. 3 vols. Paris, 1932.
Delécluze, E. *Souvenirs de soixante ans*. Paris, 1822.
Dickens, Charles. *Memoirs of Joseph Grimaldi*. London, 1884.
Diderot, Denis. *Oeuvres complètes*. Paris, 1875. Vol. 8.
Disher, Maurice Willson. *Clowns and Pantomimes*. London, 1925.
Dumas, Alexandre. *Souvenirs dramatiques*. 2 vols. Paris, 1868.
Eaton, W. P. *The Actor's Heritage*. Boston: Atlantic Monthly Press, n.d.
Escudier, Marie et Léon. *Vie et aventures des cantatrices célèbres*. Paris, 1856.
Frichet, Henri. *Le Cirque et les Forains*. Tours, 1898.
Fromageot, P. *La Foire Saint Germain*. Paris, n.d.
Frost, Thomas. *Circus Life and Circus Celebrities*. London, 1873.
——— *The Old Showmen and the Old London Fairs*. London, 1874.
Garat, D. J. *Mémoires historiques du XVIIIe siècle*. 2 vols. Paris, 1821.
Gautier, Théophile. *Histoire du romantisme*. Paris, 1874.
Gevel, C. *La Censure théâtrale sous la Restauration*. Paris, 1913.
Gildon, Charles. *Life of Betterton*. London, 1810.
Grimm, Baron de. *Correspondance littéraire, philosophique et critique*, adressée à un souverain d'Allemagne, depuis 1753, jusqu'en 1769. Par le Baron de Grimm et par Diderot. 16 vols. Paris 1813.
Harel, J. B. *Dictionnaire des théâtres*. Paris, 1836.
Hautecloque, G. *Les Représentations dramatiques dans les collèges de l'Artois*. Abbeville, 1888.
Hazlitt, Wm. *Complete Works*. London, 1934. Vol. 3.
Hedgcock, F. A. *Garrick et ses amis français*. Paris, 1911.
Héroard, Jean. *Journal de Jean Héroard sur l'enfance et la jeunesse de Louis XIII (1601-1628)*. 2 vols. Paris, 1868.
Heulhard, A. *La Foire Saint Laurent*. Paris, 1878.
Janin, Jules. *Histoire du théâtre à quatre sous*. Paris, 1832.
——— *Almanach de la littérature, du théâtre et des Beaux Arts*. 3 vols. Paris, 1853-69.
Jusserand, J. J. *Shakespeare en France*, Paris, 1898.
Laurence, W. J. *The Elizabethan Playhouse*. Stratford upon Avon, 1912.
Lennox, William P. *Celebrities I Have Known*. 4 vols. London, 1876-7.
——— *Plays, Players, and Playhouses*. 2 vols. London, 1881.
Leroux, Hugues. *Les Jeux du cirque et la vie foraine*. Paris, 1889.
Macready, William. *Reminiscences*, ed. Sir F. Pollock. London, 1876.
——— *Diaries of Wm. C. Macready*, ed. W. Toynbee. London, 1912.

Magnin, Charles. *Causeries et méditations . . . litteraires.* 2 vols. Paris, 1834.
—— *Histoire des marionnettes.* Paris, 1834.
Marshal, Thos. *Lives of the Most Celebrated Actors and Actresses.* London, 1848.
Martin, Sir Theodore. *Helena Faucit, Lady Martin.* London, 1900.
Mathews, Mrs. Anne. *Memoirs of Charles Mathews, Comedian.* 4 vols. 2nd ed.: London, 1839.
Merle, T. *Le Monstre et le Magicien: Mélodrame féerie en trois actes à grand spectacle par MM. Merle et Antony.* Paris, 1826.
Nansouty, Max. *Les Trucs au théâtre.* Paris, 1909.
Niklaus, Thelma. *Harlequin.* New York, 1956.
Nougaret, P. J. *Les Spectacles de la foire.* 7 vols. Paris, 1778–80.
—— *Les Spectacles des foires.* 2 vols. Paris, 1774 et seq.
—— *Histoire des chevaux célèbres.* Paris, 1810.
Parfait, C. *Dictionnaire des théâtres.* 7 vols. Paris, 1756.
Parfait, C. et F. *Mémoires pour servir à l'histoire de la foire.* 2 vols. Paris, 1743.
Partridge, Eric. *The French Romantics' Knowledge of English Literature (1820–1848).* Paris, 1924.
Pearce, Charles. *Mme Vestris and her Times.* London, 1923.
Péricaud, Louis. *Le Théâtre des funambules.* Paris, 1897.
—— *Théâtre des petits comédiens de S. A. S. Monseigneur le comte de Beaujolais.* Paris, 1909.
Perrodil, Edouard. *Monsieur Clown.* Paris, 1889.
Perwick, William. *The Dispatches of Wm. Perwick English Agent in Paris,* ed. for the Royal Historical Society by Mr. B. Curran. London, 1903.
Porel, Paul et Monval, Georges. *L'Odéon: Histoire administrative, anecdotique et littéraire du second théâtre français 1818–1853.* Paris, 1882.
Porte, L'Abbé de la. *Calendrier historique des théâtres de l'Opéra et des Comédies Françaises et Italiennes et des foires.* Paris, 1752.
Rémy, Tristan. *Les Clowns.* Paris, 1945.
Riccoboni, L. *Réflexions sur le théâtre.* Paris, 1738.
Ricord, Alexandre (aîné). *Les Fastes de la Comédie Française.* 2 vols. Paris, 1821–2.
Royer, A. *Histoire universelle du théâtre.* Paris, 1870.
Sand, Maurice. *Masques et bouffons (Théâtre Italien).* 2 vols. Paris, 1860.
Sevelinges, C. D. *Le Rideau levé.* Paris, 1818.
Strehly, G. *L'Acrobatie et les Acrobates.* Paris, 1903.
Texte, J. *Jean-Jacques Rousseau et les origines du cosmopolitisme littéraire: Etude sur les relations littéraires de la France et de l'Angleterre au XVIIIe siècle.* Paris, 1909.
Vandenhoff, George. *Leaves From an Actor's Note-book.* London, 1865.
Vaux, Baron de. *Ecuyers et écuyères.* Paris, 1893.
Victor, B. *History of the Stage and Letters.* 3 vols. London, 1730–71.

NEWSPAPERS AND PERIODICALS

Almanach des spectacles depuis le commencement du 19me siècle. Antoine Coupart. Paris, 1823.

Almanach des spectacles de KYZ. 1818-25.
Album, L'. 1822.
Bentley's Miscellany. Volumes VII and VIII. London, 1830 et seq.
Coulisses, Les. 1842-.
Courrier des théâtres, Le (later became *Courrier des spectacles, Le*). 1822-55.
Court Journal, The. London, 1833.
Figaro. 1829.
France théâtrale, La. 1844-5.
Gentleman's Magazine, The. May, 1890.
Globe, Le. 1822-30.
Illustration, L'. November, 1918.
Incorruptible, L'. 1827-9.
Journal des débats, Le. 1844-5.
Journal de Galignani, Le. 1822.
Journal des théâtres, Le. 1845.
Mercure de France, Le. 1827-8.
Messager, Le. 1844-5.
Minerve française, La. 1818.
Miroir, Le. 1822.
Pandore, La. 1822-30.
Plume, La. 1890.
Réveil, Le. 1822.
Revue britannique, La. 1877.
Revue germanique, La. Mai-juin, 1905.
Revue de littérature comparée. 1937.
Revue de Paris, La. 1839.
Revue et chronique parisienne, 1818.
Revue et gazette des théâtres, La. 1865-7.
Revue des théâtres, La. 1855.
Spectacles de Paris, Les. 1754-78.
Tableau des théâtres. *L'Almanach nouveau pour l'année* 1748.
Théâtre, Le. 1855-63.
Union, L'. 1859.

Index of Proper Names

ABBOT, William, 73, 74, 77, 78, 79, 80, 82, 85, 93, 94, 159, 161, 163
Addison, Joseph, 70
Agoust, 141, 142
Alard, Charles, 9, 167
Alingham, 73
Ancelot, Mme V., 112
Angoulême, Duchesse de, 33
Archer, 98
Archer, William, 113
Armand, 28
Arnal, 119
Arnold, 53
Astley, John, 30, 31, 35
Astley, Philip, 29–34, 36, 126, 127, 128, 161, 164
Astley, Mrs. Philip, 30
Auber, D. F., 97
Auriol, Baptiste, 137
Auriol, *père*, 126, 132, 134, 137

BADDELY, Robert, 38
Banks, 4, 5, 157, 161, 167
Banville, T., 142
Baptiste, *cadet*, 81
Barbier, 111
Barnes, James, 130, 131, 132
Barnet, Morris, 155
Baron, Michel, 13
Baron, Mme Michel, 13, 167
Baron, *fils*, 37
Barton, 59, 60
Bates (or Beates), 29
Baudelaire, Charles, 136, 161
Baxter, Richard, 12, 13, 14, 15, 16, 18, 19, 144, 159, 161, 167, 168
Beaumarchais, 13, 40, 45
Beauvalet, 110
Beethoven, L. von, 91
Belling, Tom, 146, 147
Bennett, G., 103, 115, 116, 117
Berlioz, Hector, 91, 92, 98, 99, 100, 113
Bernard, Eric, 72
Bernhardt, Sarah, 152, 153
Bertin, aîné, 110
Betterton, Thomas, 6, 164, 167
Bibb, Joe, 143, 144
Bienfait, Nicolas, 168, 169

Blanchard, 127, 131
Blondell, 33
Boileau, N., 69
Bonner, 45
Bonneville, 44, 45
Boswell, J., 138, 139, 153
Bouffé, 134
Boulanger, L., 90
Bridge, William, 148, 149
Broadfoot, Mrs., 33
Bromley, 63
Brunet, 53, 81
Buchanan, 5
Buckingham, Duke of, 167
Bulwer Lytton, E., 102
Butt, Sir Alfred, 156
Byron, Lord, 90, 107, 121

CAIGNIEZ, Louis Charles, 69
Calderon, 70, 71
Candler, 137, 139
Canning, Lord, 72
Capelle, Pierre Adolphe, 69, 70
Carnivelle, 168
Castellane, M. de, 100
Catalini, Mme, 47, 48
Catelan, Comte de, 44
Cervantes, Miguel, 90
Chadwick, 140, 146, 147
Chaplin, Charles, 149, 150
Chapman, 103
Charles I, 62
Charles II, 6, 7, 62
Charles X, 132
Charmoton, 25
Chartres, Duc de, 44
Chase, Pauline, 156
Chasles, Philarète, 55
Chateaubriand, F. R., 103
Chaussée, N. de la, 39
Chevalier, Maurice, 149
Chocolat, 148, 151, 152, 153, 154, 155
Cibber, Colley, 37
Cibber, Theo., 37
Cibber, Mrs. Theo., 37, 168
Clairon, Mlle, 38, 39, 40
Clark, Joseph, 167

Cleveland, Miss, 116, 117
Cole (or Calcroft), 50, 51
Collé, Charles, 39, 42
Colman, George, 52, 65
Comte, 53
Condillac, 41
Cooke, Thomas, 55, 56, 67, 130, 131
Corneille, Pierre, 58, 69, 70, 93
Coupart, Antoine, 66
Cowley, Mrs. Hannah, 79
Coyne, 115

DALEY, J. Austen, 156
Dante, 90
Darly, Maurice, 122
Davis, 35
Debureau, Jean Gaspard, 128, 129, 131, 132, 142, 143
De Castro, John, 127
Delacroix, Eugène, 87, 90, 91, 129
Delaroche, Paul, 91, 103, 110
Delamain (or de la Meyne), Henry, 20, 168
De la Place, 40
Delécluze, E. J., 72, 76
Denis, Achille, 118, 119
Derwin, 127
Desgranges, 124, 125
Deschamps, Emile, 87, 162
Desmond, Fred, 142
Desserre, 62
Devaux (or Desvaux), 167
Devéria, Achille, 90
Devisse, 38
Dickens, Charles, 104, 121
Dickons, Mrs., 48
Diderot, Denis, 39, 41
Doligny, 74
Doré, Gustave, 119
Dorneval, 14, 17, 167
Dorval, Mme, 100, 101, 102
Dryden, John, 63
Dubreuil, 115, 116, 117
Ducis, Jean François, 71, 73
Ducrow, Andrew, 32, 33, 34, 35, 121, 127
Dumanoir, M, 102
Dumas, Alexandre, 86, 87, 102, 104, 105, 107, 112, 113, 121
Dumesnil, Mlle, 39

EDWARD, George, 156
Ellar, Tom, 130, 131
Eugénie, Empress, 137

FAIRFIELD, 51
Faucit, Helena, 103, 104, 105, 106, 107, 108, 109, 110, 111, 112, 114, 159

Favart, 21, 22, 23, 38
Ferguson, 21
Feron, Mrs., 48
Feydeau, 60
Flexmore, James, 134
Foote, Maria, 73, 75, 79, 81, 82, 159
Foote, Samuel, 38
Footitt, George, 148, 150, 151, 152, 153, 155
Fox, Lord, 37
Franconi, 28, 32, 33, 34, 35, 36, 127, 129
Fresne, M. de, 103, 110, 112, 114
Fuller, Loie, 149
Fuzelier, 13, 14, 17, 167
Fye, A. Ruin de, 115, 117, 118

GARGUILLE, Gaultier, 3
Garrick, David, 38-44, 71, 78, 111, 112, 163, 168, 169
Garthwaeth, 127
Gaskill, Miss, 60
Gautier, T., 121
Genlis, Mme de, 44
George III, 62
George IV, 37
George, Mlle, 72, 110, 116
German, 168
German, Frederica, 168
Gide, André, 71
Glen, Isabella, 155
Gobert, 56
Goethe, 70
Goldoni, 71
Gontard, Jean, 132
Goodman, C., 37
Greace (or Grice), 144, 145, 146, 151, 152
Grenier, 91
Grimaldi, Joe, 127, 132, 134
Grimm, F. M., 39, 41
Grock, 164
Guyon, Jimmy, 147, 148, 151

HALEVY, 110
Hamoche, 16
Hanlons, 141, 142, 143, 153, 156
Hardy, A., 159
Harris, 45
Hartley, Mrs., 37
Haughton, 18, 168
Hayden, Billy, 145, 146, 151, 161
Haynes, Joe, 6, 7, 19, 167
Helvétius, 39
Hendrick, 21
Henri IV, 4
Henriot, Emile, 157
Hill, Benson, 50, 51
Hill, Lord, 52

INDEX

Hoffman, André, 108
Holbach, Baron d', 39, 40
Holcroft, Thomas, 44, 45, 169
Hogarth, William, 26
Huet, 93
Hugo, Victor, 43, 86, 88, 101, 107, 109, 110, 111, 113, 129
Hugounet, Paul, 135
Hume, D., 40
Hyam, 28, 29, 30, 169
Hyam, Mrs., 28, 29

IRVING, Sir Henry, 125

JANIN, Jules, 101
Joly, 54
Jonas, 169
Jonson, Ben, 5

KEAN, Edward, 53, 54, 63, 74, 75, 76, 78, 79, 80, 83, 84, 85, 87, 88, 90, 95, 96, 102, 155, 159, 163
Kelly, Fanny, 155
Kelly, Joseph, 51
Kelly, Michael, 38, 51
Kemble, Charles, 73, 75, 76, 77, 82, 100, 153, 155, 159, 162
Kemble, John, 78, 94, 103, 155
Kemp, Thomas, 133, 137, 138, 139, 144
Kempe, William, 167
Knowles, 74, 84
Kotzebue, 63, 71, 94, 96
Kuensley, 27

LAMARTINE, A. de, 86
La Pierre, 168
Laristi, 137, 138, 139
Latour, 21, 168
Laurent, Charles, 128
Laurent, Clément, 128, 129, 130
Laurent, Emile, 54, 67, 68, 72, 73, 75, 162
Laurent, Mme, 31
Lauri family, 156
Leduc, 111
Lee, 141, 143
Lekain, Henri Louis, 41, 43, 111
Lemaître, Frédéric, 34, 101, 124
Lennox, William Pitt, 49, 50
Lesage, Alain René, 13, 14, 15, 17, 167
Letourneur, Pierre, 40, 71
Lewis, G. M. (Monk), 63
Listener, 122
Liston, 51, 81
Liszt, Franz, 101
Locke, 113

Louis le Gros, 8
Louis Philippe, 109
Louis XIII, 4
Louis XIV, 10, 157
Lowe, Hudson, 158
Loyal, 148

MACKAY, J., 142
Machlin, 44
Macready, William, 54, 74, 75, 76, 77, 78, 79, 80, 83, 84, 85, 90, 91, 95, 98, 102–14, 115, 153, 155, 159, 163
Mainbray, 24, 25
Maintenon, Mme de, 10
Malibran, Mme, 84, 101
Marie Antoinette, 37
Marivaux, 40, 87
Marmontel, 40
Mars, Mlle, 65, 72, 103
Martainville, A. L., 59, 61
Martin, 35
Martin, Sir Theodore, 106
Masson, Miss, 28
Massey, Rose, 125
Mathews, 22, 168
Mathews, Charles, 51, 52, 53, 54, 55, 81, 118
Mathews, C. J., 51, 118, 119, 120, 121, 155, 161
Mathews, Tom, 133, 134, 135, 136, 161
Mathurin, Mrs., 103
Maurice, Charles, 113
Mazurier, 34, 126, 130, 132
McSwinney, Owen, 37
Medrano, 151, 154
Menken, Ada, 121, 122, 123
Merle, J. T., 55, 58, 59, 61, 66, 67
Milache, Etienne, 16
Mitchell, 103, 104, 109, 111, 114
Moke, Camille, 99
Molé, 43
Molière, 13, 58, 70
Monnet, Jean Louis, 23, 38, 40, 158
Monselet, Charles, 120
Moreau, 90
Morellet, Abbé, 39
Mozart, 91
Musset, Alfred de, 86, 87, 88

NAPOLEAN I, 58, 59, 158
Napoleon III, 137
Nicolet, Jean Baptiste, 24, 31, 126, 127, 169
Nilock, 22, 24
Nivellon, Louis, 12, 13
Nodier, Charles, 72, 85, 129, 162
Noverre, Jean Georges, 163

ORLÉANS, Duchesse d', 100
Otway, Thomas, 74
Ozières, Jacques, 167

PARSELOE, 130, 131, 137
Pearl, Cora, 123
Penley, S., 58–66, 67, 79, 98, 158, 159, 162
Penley, Miss, 60, 65, 66
Penley, Miss R., 60
Perlet, 54
Phillips, 20, 168
Picard, 80
Pichot, A. de, 72, 85
Pierson, 59
Pixérécourt, G. de, 69
Plessis, Mlle, 110
Poe, Edgar Allen, 136
Ponsard, 113
Pontou, 20, 21, 168
Potier, 53, 54, 81
Power, Tyrone, 81
Prescott, 50
Préville, 42
Prévot, Mlle, 15
Price, John, 139–40

RABRESEL, G. 167
Rabresel, Mme, 167
Racine, Jean, 58, 69, 70, 161
Rachel, 101, 103, 112, 113
Ravenscroft, 7
Raymond, 125
Razade, 29
Régnier, 104, 106, 110, 114
Renton, 18, 168
Restier, 25
Retz, 115, 116
Riancey, H. de, 114
Rich, Christopher, 19
Rich, John, 19, 37, 168
Rinner (or Riner), John, 17, 168
Ristori, Mme, 114, 115, 117, 120
Rivington, J., 44
Roberti (or Roberts), 20, 168
Robinson, Mrs., 37
Roger, 18, 168
Rolph (or Relph) Harry, 148–50
Roqueplan, Nestor, 133, 134, 135
Rowe, Nicholas, 63, 73, 74

SAINT AGNAN CHOLER, 135
Saint Eloy, 76, 82, 102
Saint Léon, Mme, 95, 96, 97
Samson, J., 112
Sand, George, 101, 111, 114

Sandham, Mrs., 22, 24, 168
Sangor, Michael, 143
Sardou, 152
Saunders (or Sanders), Billy, 29, 126
Saunders, Lucy, 30
Saurin (or Sorin), 13, 14, 167, 168
Scott, Sir Walter, 63, 66, 72, 87
Scribe, E., 80, 110
Schiller, 70, 71, 77
Sehais, Jean, 3, 167
Serle, Mrs., 107
Shakespeare, 4, 40, 44, 57, 58, 60, 61, 62, 64, 66, 69, 70, 71, 72, 74, 75, 76, 77, 78, 83, 86, 87, 88, 89, 90, 91, 92, 93, 94, 95, 96, 98, 99, 101, 104, 105, 113, 115, 160, 162, 163, 165
Shelley, Mrs., 55
Sheridan, Richard, 61, 71, 73, 74, 80, 94, 162
Simpson, Miss, 115
Smith, William, 37
Smithson, Harriet, 73, 74, 76, 77, 81, 84, 85, 88, 91, 92, 93, 97, 98, 99, 100, 101, 105, 114, 159, 163
Smithson, Joseph, 66, 67
Sothern, Edward, 124, 125
Southerne, 98
Southey, 131
Sticoti, Antonio, 41
Stendhal, 72, 85
Stuart, Sir Charles, 66, 67
Suard, Jean Baptiste, 40, 41
Suard, Mme, 40
Sue, E., 110
Swinburne, A., 121

TALMA, F. J., 48, 49, 53, 65, 71, 72, 82, 84, 155
Tasso, 90
Tate, Nahum, 78
Telocin, 169
Terry, 54, 76, 80
Thierry, Edouard, 105, 108
Tiercelin, 53
Thomassin, 18
Thomson, J., 39, 96
Torre, 26, 27
Torse, 168
Trevelyan, Hilda, 156

VALABRÈGUE, 47, 48
Vega, Lope de, 70
Vestris, Mme, 47, 48, 49, 118
Vestris, Armand, 47
Vestris, Auguste, 30, 31
Vigny, A. de, 87, 102, 110
Villemain, 72
Viollet le duc, 72

Voltaire, 40, 44, 69, 70, 71
Vondrebecke, Maurice, 9, 11
Vondrebecke, Mme, 11

WALLACK, James, 94, 95, 96, 97, 159
Wallack, William, 115, 116, 117, 159
Wallack, Mrs. William, 116, 117
Walpole, Horace, 30, 31
Ward, Genevieve, 156
Weaver, John, 19

Wellington, Lord, 50, 52, 62
West, Mrs. 94, 95, 96
Wheal, William, 139, 140
Wildman, 169
Woolton brothers, 167
Wyndham, R., 109
Wynyard, Diana, 156

YATES, Frederick, 49, 50, 51, 52, 53, 54, 68
Young, 53

www.ingramcontent.com/pod-product-compliance
Lightning Source LLC
Chambersburg PA
CBHW020412080526
44584CB00014B/1298